D1348360

GWR Steam

Uniform with this book

SOUTHERN STEAM
(second impression)
LNER STEAM
LMS STEAM

Cornish Riviera Express with Centenary stock (1935) in Sonning Cutting
N° 6000 *King George V* (from a painting by Victor Welch)

GWR STEAM

by

O. S. NOCK, B.Sc., C.Eng.
F.I.C.E., F.I.Mech.E.

DAVID & CHARLES : NEWTON ABBOT

ISBN 0 7153 5051 8

COUNTY COPY

COPYRIGHT NOTICE

© O. S. NOCK 1972

All rights reserved. No part of this publication
may be reproduced, stored in a retrieval system,
or transmitted, in any form or by any means,
electronic, mechanical, photocopying, recording
or otherwise, without the prior permission of
David & Charles (Publishers) Limited

HERTFORDSHIRE
COUNTY LIBRARY
625.261
5639504

Set in 11 on 12-point Baskerville
and printed in Great Britain
by W. J. Holman Limited Dawlish
for David & Charles (Publishers) Limited
South Devon House Newton Abbot Devon

Contents

Illustrations

Illustrations

Illustrations

Preface

I F the sheer weight of letterpress devoted to it is anything to go by, the Great Western must be the most popular of railways. Over the past quarter of a century, in response to the requests of various publishers, I myself have contributed to no fewer than eight books dealing exclusively with Great Western matters; and when one looks to the works of Mac-Dermot, W. G. Chapman and the detailed histories of the various groups of locomotives published by the RCTS it could indeed be wondered if anything was left to be said. But then the existing trilogy of books that I have written on the steam locomotives of the other main line companies in the grouping era—Southern, LNER and LMS—would have been sadly incomplete without something about the Great Western, to complete the picture; and in re-reading those companion volumes and studying the Great Western saga in broad perspective the shape of this book began to take place.

There is no doubt that the fame of the four cylinder 4–6–0s has tended to dominate the Great Western scene, in its popular appeal, and to obscure the extent to which Swindon was overwhelmingly attached to the two-cylinder 'engine', and equally to the Stephenson link motion. There were excellent reasons for this attachment, far removed from any supine attitude that could not think beyond Churchward. Then again, behind the aura of 'Stars', 'Castles' and 'Kings' there lay the somewhat astonishing fact that more than one-third of the total locomotive stock consisted of 0–6–0 tank engines! In 1922, at the time of grouping, large numbers of these could almost be claimed as of mid- rather than late-Victorian vintage. And when it comes to locomotives of that period there is the remarkable case of the Dean Goods, the outstanding performances of which had a considerable influence upon at least one facet of British Railways' locomotive development.

In this book, therefore, while paying yet another tribute to the express passenger engines the names of which are still carried high in metaphorical neon lights, I have tried to present a broader picture, arising in large measure from the warm friendship that was extended to me by men of every estate, from the most senior officers to drivers and firemen on the humblest of duties. My indebtedness to F. W. Hawksworth, K. J. Cook and R. A. Smeddle is mentioned at many points in the text. Equally there have been the running superintendents F. C. Hall, W. N. Pellow and H. E. A. White, and many of their locomotive inspectors, who have been such pleasant and informative companions in many thousands of miles riding on the footplate. There have been days in the great divisional centres, like Wolverhampton and Newton Abbot; days in the drawing office and works at Swindon, and above all the privilege of riding in the dynamometer car with Sam Ell and his splendid team of engineers on many important test runs. Through those privileges I can, in all modesty, say that on several occasions I have seen Great Western history made.

This book is thus mainly about engineering, and the end-product of that engineering in the behaviour of locomotives out on the road. It would have been impossible, in the space available, to have produced anything in the way of a definitive history. In any case this has most adequately and admirably been done already. But I have known the GWR well since I first took up residence in the London area, in 1921, and I have not resisted the temptation to allow a few personal reminiscences to intrude into the story. It was at first thought that the book should end at the time of nationalisation; but the exercise of such a guillotine would have robbed the later part of the story of much of its significance, and so the concluding chapters contain accounts of the monumental work of Sam Ell, under the stimulating leadership of Alfred Smeddle.

And then, just when one thought the story was ended, for all time, the enterprise of H. P. Bulmer Ltd of Hereford, and the co-operation of the British Railways Board enabled the *King George V* to take the road once again at the head of a revenue-earning train. The astonishing demonstrations of interest and affection that this round trip created were just one more manifestation of the popularity of the Great Western, even though the company itself ceased to exist twenty-four years ago.

Lastly, I am, as always, deeply grateful to Olivia my wife for her help in typing the MSS, and for her never failing attention to all incidentals in preparing the script.

Silver Cedars   O. S. NOCK
High Bannerdown   November 1971
Batheaston
BATH

CHAPTER 1

A Survey in 1922

IN the first returns of the locomotive stock of the British railways since the end of World War I the Great Western showed a total of 3,119, in the somewhat surprising proportion of 1,389 tender and 1,730 tank engines. Moreover, of the latter no fewer than 1,100—*one thousand one hundred*—were 0–6–0 tank engines. One thinks so instinctively of the Great Western of that period as a line steeped in the Churchward standardisation precepts that it comes as something of a surprise to realise how little towards full standardisation matters had actually progressed. At the time of Churchward's retirement at the end of 1921, a famous composite photograph issued from Swindon showed the 'standard' locomotives to be contained in ten classes, as shown in Table 1.

TABLE 1

Wheel arrangement	Class	Number of locomotives
4–6–2	'No 111'	1
4–6–0	'Star'	61
4–6–0	'Saint'	77
4–4–0	'County'	40
2–6–0	'43XX'	207
2–8–0	'47XX'	1
2–8–0	'28XX'	84
4–4–2T	'22XX'	30
2–6–2T	'31XX'	81
2–8–0T	'42XX'	95

These mustered a total of only 677, or 21.7 per cent of the

12

total stock. At the same time it must be borne in mind that there also existed the light 2–6–2 tank, or '45XX' class, which was definitely a standard though not having the otherwise standard 18½in by 30in cylinders. At the time of Churchward's retirement there were 55 of these smart little engines in traffic.

Looking now at the 1920 passenger locomotive stock in general, it included no fewer than 78 of the 2–4–0 type, and 368 4–4–0s. Of these latter a total of 328 were non-standard, and mainly of the 'Camel' and 'Atbara' classes and their derivatives. There were also the three De Glehn compound 'Atlantics', all by that time fitted with Great Western standard boilers. The 78 2–4–0s included in the first post-war returns were of various Dean designs, but were notable and unique in British locomotive history including among their numbers some of the only British 2–4–0s ever to be superheated. This leads me on to another and less familiar aspect of Churchward's modernisation policy. While it was obvious that the broad principles of design embodied in eight out of the ten 'standard' classes—namely, two outside cylinders, long-travel valves, taper boilers, and high steam pressure—could not be applied throughout the entire 3,000-odd locomotives of the GWR stud, a considerable degree of standardisation could be, and was, effected in respect of detail parts and cab fittings. In general however the programme of standardisation was no more than just under way by the time Churchward retired.

TABLE 2

Assorted 2–4–0s of Dean classes	78
'3521' class of 5ft 4–4–0s	39
'Armstrong' class 4–4–0s	4
'Duke' class 4–4–0s	40
'Badminton' class 4–4–0s	20
'Bulldog' class 4–4–0s	156
'Atbara' class 4–4–0s	29
'City' class 4–4–0s	20
'Flower' class 4–4–0s	20
De Glehn Compound 4–4–2s	3
Assorted 0–6–0s of Armstrong and Dean classes	435
The 'Aberdare' class 2–6–0s	81

Apart from the standard engines with two outside cylinders it is necessary to take more than a passing glance at the substantial *bloc* of 925 non-standard tender engines, made up as shown (Table 2) in the stud of 1920.

At the time of the 1920 return, scrapping of the inside cylinder 4–4–0s had scarcely begun. One of the 'Atbaras' No 3382 *Mafeking*, had been damaged beyond repair in the accident at Henley-in-Arden in 1911, but the only other example of a 4–4–0 scrapped was one of the '3521' class, which were conversions from tank engines. A considerable degree of standardisation had been attained between the five original classes of express passenger 4–4–0s, bringing the 'Armstrong', 'Badminton', 'Atbara' and 'Flower' classes into one group named collectively 'Flowers', while the 'Cities' having identical cylinders and motion had slightly larger boilers. The former group had the Swindon No 2 standard, and consisted of bringing the three older classes into line with the 'Flowers', while the 'Cities' had the No 4 boiler, as used on the standard outside-cylinder 'Counties', on the 2–6–0s and certain of the large standard tank engines.

Having regard to the fact that on Churchward's retirement there were only 179 'standard' express passenger engines on the line it will be evident that the older and non-standard 4–4–0s were still called upon for much work of a main line character. At the time of grouping the Great Western had less than 150 express passenger 4–6–0s, despite the extensive and far-flung main line network, whereas at the same time the London and North Western Railway had 275 superheater 4–6–0s and an efficient stud of about 150 superheater 4–4–0s of a tractive ability at least equal to that of the Great Western 'Counties'. The comparative figures of first-line passenger locomotives on these two major railways was thus 425 on the North Western, and only 179 on the Great Western. In addition to the 'City' and 'Flower' groups the Great Western had, of course, an extremely useful second-line stud in the 156 5ft 8in 4–4–0s of the 'Bulldog' class, with the Swindon No 2 standard boiler, and cylinders and motion identical to those of the 'Cities' and 'Flowers'.

The general pattern of express passenger locomotive working in the 1920-2 period may be briefly reviewed next,

14

though it is important to emphasise that the following is a general picture, and one to which individual observers might have noted exceptions. The four-cylinder 4–6–0s of the 'Star' class were stationed only at Old Oak Common, Stafford Road, (Wolverhampton), Newton Abbot and Laira (Plymouth). They covered practically the whole of the Birmingham and north expresses, between Paddington and Wolverhampton, and the double–home West of England turns from Paddington to Torquay and Plymouth. The two-cylinder 'Saint' class 4–6–0s were stationed mostly at Bristol, Cardiff, Exeter, Landore (Swansea), Shrewsbury and Worcester. They did not have a complete monopoly of the South Wales trains because certain London turns were worked by 'Stars'. Similarly, one of the two-hour Bristol expresses formed part of a London–Plymouth double-home turn and was almost invariably worked by a 'Star'.

The Bristol 'Saints' worked most of the west to north expresses, both south–westwards to Plymouth and northwards to Shrewsbury by the Severn Tunnel route. The through service between Wolverhampton and the West of England was almost exclusively in the hands of 4–4–0 locomotives of the 'County' class on the section north of Bristol, these being the heaviest Great Western locomotives permitted to run over the Midland Railway between Yate and Standish Juncton. South of Bristol these trains were hauled by 'Saint' class engines. During the period of the summer service some reliefs and extra trains over the Birmingham–Bristol line were run by inside cylinder 4–4–0s, and these engines were used sometimes for piloting the 'Counties' with very heavy loads. 4–4–0 locomotives were extensively used on the secondary express services from Bristol, including those to South Wales, to Weymouth and to Salisbury with the through Portsmouth trains. One found the inside cylinder 4–4–0s on the further sections of the principal main lines such as north of Wolverhampton to Chester and Birkenhead, west of Cardiff and Swansea, and available as bank engines at Newton Abbot and Plymouth.

The Paddington–Weymouth trains were for long a preserve of 4–4–0 locomotives. Some of the heavier services were worked by 'Counties', but 'Flowers' and 'Bulldogs' did most of the work. On the other hand, the Cornish main line, which at one time was worked almost exclusively by 'Bulldogs', had been taken over by the standard '43XX' class 2–6–0s, except for an occasional trip by a Laira, or Newton Abbot 4–6–0. The inside cylinder 4–4–0s were much in evidence at Oxford, and they worked through trains on the Newcastle–Bournemouth service between Banbury and Basingstoke. The three French compounds were also at Oxford, and one of them was usually to be seen on the 9.45am express from Paddington. *The Great Bear* was at Old Oak Common and led a somewhat placid existence on the less important Bristol expresses.

Turning from express passenger to mixed traffic engines, the '43XX' class 2–6–0, although the last of the standard engines to be introduced, proved a great success, and by the end of 1921 it was the most numerous of all the standard classes. Its numbers had topped the 200 mark, and additions were then being made to the class. The heavy inside-cylindered 2–6–0s of the 'Aberdare', or '26XX' class were rarely seen outside South Wales. There was plenty of work for all 81 of them in local freight and mineral service, leaving the long-haul jobs from Severn Tunnel eastwards to the standard '28XX' class 2–8–0s. The Great Western had avoided the intermediate step passed through by many of the British railways in progressing from six-coupled freight engines, going straight from the 0–6–0 to the 2–8–0, without building engines of the 0–8–0 type.

After World War I the Great Western took over no less than 100 of the standard ROD 2–8–0s of Great Central design, built to the order of the Ministry of Munitions. The British railways of pre–grouping days in their independence of outlook did not take kindly to locomotives, or any other form of equipment, designed by different railways, and the London and North Western, which also acquired a number of the ROD 2–8–0s, did not keep them long. In this respect it is certainly a tribute to the Great Central design that they became a virtual standard on the Great Western; they were equipped with Great Western fittings, and put in many years of hard and reliable work. They retained their GCR-type boilers throughout. There were probably structural reasons why the Great Western standard No 1 boiler, used on the '28XX' class could not be applied to them. The ROD engines became

Page 17. (above) *The pioneer two-cylinder 4–6–0, recognisable from its cylinder mounting: No 2900* William Dean *on up South Wales express near Reading; (below) another historic 4–6–0: No 2971* Albion, *on Penzance–Aberdeen express descending Dainton bank*

Page 18. (above) *Dean double-framed 2–4–0, '3206' class of 1889, as fitted with domed Belpaire boiler; (centre) a one-time 7ft 2–2–2 of 1869 vintage, as rebuilt as 0–6–0 in 1900-2. The last of this class was not withdrawn until 1920; (below) Armstrong double-framed 0–6–0, as fitted with later standard Belpaire domed boiler*

the '30XX' class on the Great Western, and the acquisition of these engines just after the war, while greatly relieving the pressure upon the freight locomotive stud, enabled Swindon's new construction to be concentrated on 2–6–0 mixed traffic engines, and heavy tank engines for use in South Wales. These latter are referred to in some detail later.

A most important group of non-standard locomotives was that embodying the 435 0–6–0 tender engines. As on most British railways of that period the 0–6–0 was the maid of all work in secondary service, capable of any kind of freight haulage, and of light passenger work. One class in particular, the Dean '2301' series, at one time mustered no fewer than 260 engines. Their numbers originally ran from 2301 to 2360, and from 2381 to 2580. By the time of grouping however their number had been reduced to 232. Twenty of them, Nos 2491 to 2510 had been rebuilt at 2–6–2 tanks before World War I, and of the 62 which were sent abroad in 1917 seven never came back. The remaining one, No 2448, was so badly damaged in the collision at Thingley Junction, Chippenham, in 1907, that she was subsequently scrapped. The class as a whole were such economical and reliable engines that they became, virtually, one of the GWR standards. The majority of them were superheated, and in the Collett era a number of new classes were developed from them, and are described in Chapter 8. The continued prowess of the '2301' class itself is the subject of special comment later in this book.

In 1921 when I went to London to commence my engineering studies the one and only 5ft 8½in 2–8–0 No 4700 had recently been fitted with a large boiler, in replacement of the Standard No 1 originally used, and at that time the engine was in regular passenger service. She was in a curious link of four locomotives that included No 111 *The Great Bear*, and two 4-6-0s. They had some fairly humdrum duties, and on one of my earliest photographic visits to Paddington I remember being delighted to catch No 4700 on the 10.45am Gloucester and Cheltenham express. Unfortunately the 'snap' that I then secured is not of good enough quality to be reproduced here. Mr Gordon Tidey managed to photograph *The Great Bear* on the same train and his result is reproduced facing page 34. The big engines went no further than Swindon

19

B

on this job, though at a later date it became the outward working to Gloucester for the Old Oak Common engine returning on the Cheltenham Flyer. At that time engines were changed at Swindon on a number of expresses, including the 4.30pm Plymouth, which regularly changed from the Old Oak 4–6–0 to a Swindon 'Saint' at Swindon.

At the period just around the grouping, tank engine workings on the GWR were of great interest. The enormous stud of small-powered six-wheelers was dispersed all over the line. It would take whole chapters to describe the workings in any detail, but one found 0–6–0 saddle tanks, and pannier tanks on shunting work at almost every large centre. Many of these engines were, in 1922-5, very smartly turned out with the copper caps of their chimneys once again unearthed from beneath the layer of wartime black, and their dome covers once again polished. On the country branches 2–4–0 and 0–4–2 tanks of varying vintages trundled ancient four- and six-wheeled stock, some of it repainted in chocolate and cream; while many of these branch line engines were equipped for auto-train working. It is important to appreciate that in those years the renewal of the six-wheeled tank engine stock had not yet begun, and that all the engines involved in branch line and shunting duties were of Dean or Armstrong vintage.

On numerous branch line duties the steam rail motor cars were active. Workings that I remember particularly were those on the Basingstoke branch from Reading, and that on the Calne branch from Chippenham. The latter included at least one interesting main line working. It was an era when great store was set upon through carriage services, and at that time the 4.30pm and 6.30pm expresses from Paddington both detached slip coaches at Chippenham. From both these trains the slip coach was taken forward to Bath, thus providing an excellent service from London to Corsham, Box and Bathampton. And in each case the slip coach was attached to a steam rail motor car running the local service between Chippenham and Bath. Passengers for Corsham, for example, would come down from London non-stop to Chippenham on the 6.30pm from Paddington—and then proceed, admittedly at the slow speed of the 'motor trains' without change of carriage. The only disadvantage was that passengers in slip coaches had no access to dining cars. I never took any detailed timings of the rail motor cars, but they always seemed unconscionably slow. My impression is that they rarely reached as much as 45mph. When I was working at Chippenham in the summer of 1926 I used often to cycle out to Thingley Junction to photograph the 4.30pm from Paddington; and then, not long after she had come tearing past, frequently hauled by No 2923 *Saint George*, the 'motor' rail car would follow, making heavy weather of it, with two trailers, one the 'slip brake' off the 4.30pm.

Of the Victorian-age six-wheeled tank engines however, by far the most remarkable in their performance were the little 2–4–0s. These were of varying dates and origins, but I have particular memories of those on the London suburban services in the late nineteen-twenties. Of the Churchward standard types only the 4–4–2 'County' tanks were in regular service in the London area, and these were used mainly on the outer residential trains to Reading and Henley. The shorter distance trains, of which there were many, were nearly all worked by the little 2–4–0s. I was living at Ealing for a time, and used to travel almost daily by one of the through trains to the City. This was worked by a 2–4–0 tank to Bishops Road, where engines were changed and a Metropolitan electric locomotive took over. The train was always one of the six-coach, close-coupled, semi-elliptical sets built specially for the Metropolitan service. It was packed each morning, and cannot have weighed much less than 200 tons. Yet the way those little engines got away was amazing. With the lever-reverse full-forward they would pound away for the first hundred yards or so from Acton; then steam was shut off while the driver brought the lever back a few notches, then away again, usually to touch about 50mph before we slowed for the crossover to the Hammersmith and City Line by Subway Junction. Unfortunately I have not kept a record of the many individual engines concerned, but it did not seem to matter which of them was put on. The running was wonderfully consistent—so consistent indeed that I plotted a standard graph that was used in making some calculations on the spacing of colour light signals for obtaining maximum density of service with small powered steam locomotives.

21

They were extremely pretty little engines, yet it is strange to recall that as comparatively recently as the late 1920s there were tank engines on an important commuter service in the London area that had no more than scanty open cabs. In view of the various six-wheeled tank engines that were built new during the Collett régime at Swindon it is worth recalling the dimensions of these remarkable engines. They had 16in by 24in cylinders; 5ft 2in coupled wheels, and a boiler pressure of 165lb per square inch.

Of the three Churchward standard tank engine classes, 4–4–2 or '22XX' class, 2–6–2 or '31XX' and 2–8–0 or '42XX', the first named was a straight tank engine equivalent of the 'County' class 4–4–0 express passenger engines, and having the same diameter coupled wheels, 6ft 8½in. One could understand this in the case of certain contemporary English tank engine designs, such as the Marsh '13' on the Brighton, or the various 4–4–2s on the London, Tilbury and Southend. Both these were essentially express passenger classes, built as tank engines purely for convenience. But the Great Western '22XX's were suburban train engines, admittedly required to do fast work. One can only assume that when they were built the suitability of 5ft 8½in diameter coupled wheels for that kind of duty was not fully appreciated. The 'County tanks', as they were usually known, differed from their express passenger counterparts in having the smaller of the two standard boilers fitted to four-coupled engines. This was the No 2, as used on all the inside-cylinder 4–4–0s except the 'Cities'. These had the No 4, which was standard on the 'County' class 4–4–0s, and on the 2–6–2 tanks of the '31XX' class. These latter were to become the progenitors of a very large family of smaller boilered engines of the same general design; they were originally conceived as short-haul, main line freight engines, primarily for use in South Wales.

Another class of passenger tank engine must be particularly mentioned; this was the '36XX' 2–4–2, and was to the suburban passenger stud what the 'Aberdare' 2–6–0s were to the heavy main line freight—in other words a half-way house between Dean, and the full Churchward standard types with outside cylinders. The earliest examples of the '36XX' class originally had parallel domeless boilers like the 'Atbaras' and

'Camels'; but in 1921 when they were familiar to me on the
suburban services around Birmingham I think most of them
by then had tapered boilers. They were smart little engines,
but lacked the power and free-running qualities of the
Churchward standard types. There was one other isolated
passenger tank engine that Churchward probably intended to
be the prototype of a standard class, with outside cylinders,
No 4600. This curious little engine, which had cylinders 17in
diameter by 24in stroke, and coupled wheels 5ft 8in diameter,
was built at a time when wheels smaller than 6ft 8½in were
not considered suitable for fast passenger working. There is
no doubt however that the production of the '43XX' class of
main line 2–6–0, the last of the large standard types of the
Churchward régime proper, upset many of the long-cherished
ideas prevailing at Swindon. They proved so fast and steady
running that henceforth it was the 2–6–2 rather than the four-
coupled tank engines that were developed for fast passenger
working, and the little '4600' remained the only one of her
kind.

In my earliest post-war observations, just before and just
after grouping, the big 2–6–2 tanks of the '31XX' class were
still mostly engaged on freight, and in main line bank engine
work. They were much in demand as pilots through the
Severn Tunnel, both for passenger and heavy mineral trains,
and a few of them were stationed at Newton Abbot for assist-
ing over the very severe gradients of the South Devon line.
During the heaviest of the summer traffic these engines shut-
tled back and forth between Newton Abbot and Brent, and
one could often see the same engine double-heading two or
even three trains in the same day. To save engine mileage the
Newton bankers usually went no farther than Brent. It was
to avoid stalling on Dainton or Rattery bank rather than to
save time that the bank engines were used, because on many
of the long-distance expresses the extra stops at Newton and
Brent involved some *loss* of time, however much faster the
banks were climbed with two engines on. When Laira engines
were used for piloting down expresses they worked through to
Plymouth, and the time saved by avoidance of the stop at
Brent was substantial. The Laira pilots were usually 4–4–0s
of the 'Duke' or 'Bulldog' class.

A Survey in 1922

The neighbourhood of Newton Abbot is a good place to introduce those remarkable engines, the '45XX' class small 2-6-2 tanks. Although they were not shown on the well-known composite photograph of the GWR standard classes, they were in every way a standard, though not having any of the major components, such as the boiler, or cylinders interchangeable with any of the larger standard types. At the time of grouping there were fifty-five of them. They are now so well known, with some preserved and at least one in regular service on the Dart Valley Railway, that I need not dwell upon their salient characteristics at this stage Instead, some notes on their work at that period will no doubt prove of interest. They were designed specially for branch line working where maximum axle loads were limited, and where increasing loads were demanding a locomotive of considerably greater power than the Armstrong and Dean six-wheelers. There were a number of such branches in Churchward's own native Devonshire, where the going was made harder by the very severe gradients. The '45XX' 2-6-2 tanks worked on the Newquay, Falmouth and St Ives branches where the formation of some of the local trains was considerably augmented by through carriages from the Cornish Riviera and other main line expresses. But one of their hardest duties was in working almost the entire service over the heavily graded Kingswear branch.

At that time, and indeed till the late 1920s, the main line express 4-6-0s were not allowed to work south of Paignton. In consequence every express going through to Kingswear had to change engines at Paignton, and matters were not exactly helped by the commencement of single-line working immediately beyond Paignton station. The present extensive sidings at Goodrington Sands did not then exist. There was not any space at Paignton for stabling coaching stock, and any that was not going forward to Kingswear had to be hauled back to Newton Abbot. The situation that developed on some Saturdays in the height of summer defies description. Train after train from London, the Midlands, and the North would take the Torquay line at Aller Junction, and what with engine changing at Paignton, trains terminating there, and congestion from the single line beyond, there was not infrequently

24

a train standing at every stop signal between Paignton and Kingskerswell.

I remember sitting on Paignton station, on one such day, waiting to meet a relative who was coming down from London by the Torbay Limited, as the 12.0 noon from Paddington was then known, while the train itself stood for more than *thirty-five minutes* at the home signal outside. In the meantime the station staff disentangled themselves from one operating knot, only to become involved in another! At midweek, with everything running reasonably to time things went smoothly enough, though the '45XX' class tank engines had to work hard in taking over the Torbay Limited. During the summer service the normal formation of this train was seven of the latest 70ft stock, about 255 tons tare, but that minimum was frequently strengthened, on Fridays to eight, nine or even ten coaches. But in my experience the '45XX' class went pedalling up those severe gradients with complete confidence.

The large standard 2–8–0 tank engines of the '42XX' class were being used almost exclusively in South Wales. They were an ideal job for working through the Severn Tunnel, and on heavy feeder services to the main line long-haul mineral trains. It was not unusual to see two heavy tank engines working coal trains through the Severn Tunnel, with a '31XX' 2–6–2 leading and a '42XX' as train engine. In cases of exceptional loading up South Wales expresses stopped at Severn Tunnel Junction to take a pilot, and to obviate any chance of stalling, through slipping on the eastern ascent. The pilot would be a '31XX' and it was usually the practice for the engine to work through to Badminton. This gave a heavily-loaded train engine the chance to get away to a good restart, instead of having to start uphill from Stoke Gifford.

Such is no more than a glimpse of locomotive working on the GWR at the time of the grouping, and just afterwards. Lineside observation, wherever one might care to go, was regarded by a great variety of locomotives, except, strangely enough, in Cornwall where there was an overwhelming preponderance of '43XX' class Moguls when I first went there. In the last months before grouping, a new series of four-cylinder 4–6–0s was turned out from Swindon, named after abbeys; these were generally of the 'Star' class, but included some detailed improvements. With their appearance four years after the end of the war Great Western enthusiasts must have been reconciled to an indefinite continuation of the war-time style of finish, in plain, unlined green, with one-piece cast-iron chimneys and a complete absence of all the flashing brass and copper work that had so bedecked Great Western engines in pre-war years. The naming of these twelve engines involved one of those amusing oversights that sometimes arises when nomenclature of a highly systematised nature is adopted. Proceeding down the line and honouring one celebrated monastic 'pile' after another until the fragmentary Tresco in the Scilly Isles had been reached, it was respectfully pointed out that one of the greatest abbeys of all had apparently been forgotten—Westminster! Wales being well represented by Llanthony and Neath, to say nothing of Tintern on its borders, engine No 4069 *Margam Abbey* was chosen for renaming, and henceforth was called *Westminster Abbey*.

CHAPTER 2

The Welsh Constituents

WHILE the railway grouping which came into effect on 1 January 1923 did not affect the major locomotive policy and programme of the GWR, Swindon had the added responsibility of working an additional 740 route miles in Wales, together with the 63 miles of the Midland & South Western Junction. With these railways the GWR took over some 700 Welsh locomotives, but there was a great difference in the traffic on some of these lines. The Cambrian had considerably the greatest mileage but it ran through a rural and often mountainous country, and less than 90 locomotives were needed to work its 295 miles of route. On the other hand, the density of traffic on the Taff Vale and Barry is reflected in the fact that these two railways contributed 271 and 148 locomotives respectively to the enlarged GWR even though their route mileages were no more than 124 and 68. Of the total stud taken over no fewer than 450 were tank engines of the 0–6–2 type. This group taken collectively was a thoroughly sound lot. They were designed and worked by men who knew the local conditions in South Wales intimately. There was no need for refinements to produce speedy running, or to boost thermal efficiency by a few decimal points of one per cent. What was needed was a hard slogging machine that would stand up indefinitely to the rigours of the coal traffic, for the most part on lines that included severe gradients.

The locomotive stocks of the principal South Wales railways, taken over by the GWR in 1923, are shown in Table 3. There were, in addition, various smaller concerns that owned locomotives; but they did not present any problems so far as the future provision of motive power was concerned. The locomotive studs of the seven railways mentioned above each provide a fascinating study in themselves, in the variety and diversity both of designs and origins, but one cannot delve into such tempting fields of study in a single chapter. I am concerned here not so much with the stocks as they existed, but rather with the problems they presented to their new owners.

TABLE 3

Railway	Number of locomotives
Barry	148
Brecon & Merthyr	47
Cambrian	86
Cardiff	36
Rhondda & Swansea Bay	37
Rhymney	123
Taff Vale	271

The locomotive stock of the Barry Railway was undoubtedly the most individual, for that line was the only one that did not build large and modern 0–6–2 tanks in its last days. It went still bigger, with 0–6–4s, having already used for many years 0–8–0 tender and 0–8–2 tank engines. But first of all the comparative dimensions of the largest 0–6–2 tank engines on the Taff Vale, Brecon & Merthyr, and Rhymney Railways may be considered.

TABLE 4

Railway	Class Designation	Cylinders Diameter	Stroke	Coupled wheel ft in	BP lb/ sq in	Total wt tons
Taff Vale	A	$18\frac{1}{2}$	26	5–3	175	69
Brecon &	36–43	$18\frac{1}{2}$	26	4–6	175	67
Merthyr	45–50	18	26	5–0	175	61
Rhymney	A	18	26	$4–4\frac{1}{2}$	175	64
	R	$18\frac{1}{2}$	26	4–6	175	67
	P	18	26	5–0	175	61

28

From Table 4 it will be appreciated that the Brecon & Merthyr and the Rhymney had locomotives of very similar proportions. The two varieties of B & M 0–6–2 and the Rhymney 'R' and 'P' classes looked very much alike, except in their liveries. Both companies had slightly smaller and lighter engines for passenger service than for the heavy mineral service, with the small difference in coupled wheel diameter of 4ft 6in and 5ft 0in. In comparing these dimensions with those of the Cameron 'A' class on the Taff Vale, which like all preceding 0–6–2s of that railway were general purpose engines, it must be borne in mind that the Taff had much the easiest road of any of the South Wales lines. Its two principal routes, which joined at Pontypridd, followed the valleys of the Taff and Rhondda rivers, and in general its locomotives were not called upon for heavy collar work. But what they benefitted from in lack of gradients was amply compensated for in loads, and for many years 4ft 6½in had been the standard wheel diameter for the 0–6–2 tank engines. With the exception of 14 locomotives of the 'U' and 'U1' classes of 1895, the long series of 0–6–2 tanks, that began with the 'M' class of 1891, and finished with the '04' class of 1907 all had cylinders 17½in diameter by 26in stroke. There were no fewer than 134 in this series, distinguished in gradually increasing tractive power from the increase in boiler pressure from 140lb per sq in on class 'M' to 175lb per sq in on the '04' class.

The 'A' class, introduced by Mr Cameron in 1914 were larger and more modern looking engines, though having 5ft 3in coupled wheels against the 4ft 6½in of class '04' they had slightly less tractive effort, despite having cylinders 18½in diameter, instead of the hitherto standard 17½in. A total of 58 engines of this class was built between the years 1914 and 1921 and, with the 14 engines of classes 'U' and 'U1' saving 5ft 3in coupled wheels, made up a grand total of no less than 206 tank engines of the 0–6–2 type to be taken into Great Western stock. Another numerous class was a series of 40 tender engines of the 0–6–0 type built between 1875 and 1885, and having the seemingly standard 17½in by 26in cylinders, and coupled wheels 4ft 6½in diameter. With the exception of the 'A' class all these locomotives, tank and tender alike, were designed by Mr T. Hurry Riches, and before he began to adopt the 0–6–2 tank to the exclusion of all others, he introduced six 4–4–2 tanks in 1888-91, with 17½in by 26in cylinders and 5ft 3in coupled wheels for passenger service. The locomotives were still in service at the time of grouping, but converted for auto-train working.

Taken all round the locomotives of the Taff Vale Railway were a smart workmanlike lot, well suited to the heavy traffic of the line. The livery was a lined black, decorated with the striking coat of arms of the company. Although the 0–6–2 tank engines were to a large extent common-user, the 'A' class were remarkably free running. I have timed them myself at speeds up to 60mph. With their short chimneys and boiler mountings, and generally neat proportions, I always thought they were among the most handsome 0–6–2 tank engines ever built. The Great Western Railway made use of them after grouping, and later, when fitted with standard Swindon tapered boilers, they continued to do good work in South Wales. Apart from the 'A' class the only other Taff Vale locomotives to survive the grouping by more than about ten years were the '04' class. They had been introduced in 1907-10, and were 41 strong. They all became British Railways' property in 1948, at which time a number of them still retained their original type of boiler. On the basis of nominal tractive effort they were the most powerful engines in the Taff Vale stud. They were all vacuum fitted, though not often to be seen on passenger trains.

The Rhymney Railway requires special consideration in this brief survey of the Welsh constituents of the enlarged GWR in that it contributed the locomotive works that became the headquarters and maintenance centre of all locomotives working in South Wales. By comparison with the Taff Vale it was not a large railway, but it conveyed a heavy traffic, on steep gradients, and it had a tradition as strongly individual and as proud as any of the great main line companies of England and Scotland. Tom Hurry Riches had been the guiding spirit of the Taff Vale locomotive department for nearly forty years; the Rhymney had the incredible Cornelius Lundie, who had continued in office in the dual capacity of general manager and locomotive superintendent until he was *ninety* years of age, and it was indeed when he was a very active and forceful *eighty-five*(!) that he planned the new locomotive and carriage works at Caerphilly. The company had long outgrown its original works and running sheds at Cardiff Docks and when the decision was taken to replace them, an excellent site beside the main line at Caerphilly was chosen. Lundie took responsibility for placing contracts for the work, and the new shops opened for business in December 1901, when Lundie himself was eighty-seven years of age. Through this enterprise, however, the Rhymney Railway had a fine modern works, which the Great Western enlarged in 1926 and again in 1939.

A year after Cornelius Lundie had retired, in January 1905, C. T. Hurry Riches was appointed as locomotive superintendent. He was a son of the famous engineer of the Taff Vale, and came to South Wales direct from the Great Central works at Gorton. At the time the Caerphilly works was opened the Rhymney Railway had 105 locomotives, and of these all except 18 were double-framed saddle tanks. These latter were of three classes: 35 of the 0–6–0 type, 5 of the 2–4–2 type, and the remainder of the inevitable South Wales 0–6–2. The earlier 0–6–0s had 16½in by 24in cylinders, and the later 17½in cylinders, in common with all the 0–6–2 tanks. All these six-coupled engines of the Lundie era had 4ft 7in coupled wheels. The 2–4–2 tanks, which dated from 1890, also had 17½in by 24in cylinders, but 5ft diameter coupled wheels. These saddle tank engines were the backbone of the locomotive stud, though incorporating many individual details and variations, and one of the first tasks undertaken by Mr Riches was to design a standard boiler and cylinders that could be used on the entire range of saddle tank engines. At the time of grouping 59 out of the original 87 remained, but of that 59 two were on the duplicate list. The details of the Lundie saddletanks, as rebuilt with Riches boilers, in December 1922 were as follows:

Class J	0–6–0	9
Class K	0–6–2	46
Class L	2–4–2	2
Class L1	0–6–2	2

The two engines on the duplicate list were 0–6–0s. With the

exception of the two 'L' class 2–4–2s all the saddle tanks had the same type of boiler, a most praiseworthy effort in standardisation.

Mr Riches' own locomotives were all side tanks, and except for seven 0–6–0s were all of the 0–6–2 type. There were 53 of these latter, and they were a handsome and excellent lot. The sense of pride in the job which the Great Western itself cherished was evident to an extraordinary extent on the Rhymney Railway. Locomotives were painted a rich dark green, with black and white lining and chocolate underframes. There was a profusion of brasswork, and with each engine allocated to only one crew the condition in which they were kept was immaculate. It is known that more than one driver was in the habit of taking his wife to the sheds on Sunday afternoons to give an extra shine to the brasswork! In later years every schoolboy had heard of the new Great Western 4–6–0 *Caerphilly Castle*, but it was only the more erudite among railway enthusiasts who knew of Caerphilly Works, and of the locomotives built, and so splendidly maintained there.

The Brecon & Merthyr was another Welsh line of great individuality. Unlike the Taff Vale, the Rhymney and the other railways converging upon Newport, Cardiff and Swansea, it was not primarily a coal carrier. Its main line made a winding and exceedingly mountainous course from Newport to Brecon, and including short lengths of the Rhymney Railway, from Bargoed to Deri Junction, and of the Great Western from Newport itself to Bassaleg, over which it had running powers, this main line was 47¼ miles long. Referring more specifically to its gradients the late E. L. Ahrons suggested it was more like a toboggan run than a railway! Talybont-on-Usk in particular lies at the foot of very steep inclines. There is a continuous climb at 1 in 40 northwards to Talyllyn Junction, and southwards there is the worst incline on British railways—7 miles continuously at 1 in 38 to the northern entrance to Torpantau Tunnel. There are also numerous pitches at 1 in 40 to 1 in 110 in descending from the 1,314ft altitude of the railway summit, between Dowlais Top and Fochriw to Bassaleg, but nothing so severe as the Talybont–Torpantau incline. The density of traffic never approached that of the principal coal carriers in South Wales and, as will have been noted in Table 3, the Brecon & Merthyr possessed no more than 47 locomotives at the time of the grouping.

It was never a prosperous concern to the extent that the other railways of South Wales became, and many of its locomotives had been purchased secondhand from other railways. In 1918, for example, there were then 41 locomotives in service, and this small stock was subdivided as follows:

0–6–0	Saddle-tanks	24
0–6–2	Saddle-tanks	4
4–4–2	Side Tanks	1
2–4–0	Side Tanks	1
0–6–2	Side Tanks	11

Of these only the last mentioned had been recently built new for the Brecon & Merthyr, and these are the locomotives referred to in the comparison with the 0–6–2 tank engines of South Wales railways in Table 4 (page 28). The earliest of these dated from 1910, and all were built by Robert Stephenson & Co. The 0–6–0 saddle tanks were divided into four classes:

(a) 17in × 24in cylinders, 4ft 2½in coupled wheels, total 14
(b) 17in × 24in cylinders, 4ft 6in coupled wheels, total 2
(c) 17in × 24in cylinders, 4ft 7½in coupled wheels, total 5
(d) 17in × 26in cylinders, 5ft 0in coupled wheels, total 3

All these engines were picturesque, beautifully kept period-pieces. The most numerous of them, class (a), were the oldest and dated from 1874. The second class (b) had a Midland look about them, having the Derby shape of dome with Salter spring-balance valves superimposed. The (c) class had something of a Great Western look, but the first two were actually purchased from Kitsons in 1896, and the remaining three came from Nasmyth Wilson in 1900. The fourth variety were Great Western engines, purchased from Swindon in 1906 and 1907. The 0–6–2 saddle tanks were rather longer than the usual run of South Wales 0–6–2s, and although they had greater tank capacity they were of no greater tractive power than the later 0–6–0s. The 4–4–2 tank was of William Adams's design purchased from the London & South Western Railway, while the one side tank was the last on the active list of a class of six very pretty little engines built by Stephensons between 1888 and 1904, and looking very like the celebrated 'Metropolitan' 2–4–0 tanks of the GWR. But with no more than 16in by 24in cylinders and very modest boilers they were hardly equal to such a road as the Brecon & Merthyr, and by 1918 all but one had been taken out of traffic. Nevertheless, five out of the six survived to enter Great Western service, as GWR Nos 1402, 1412, 1452, 1458 and 1460. The line had a distinctive locomotive livery, of brick red with the panels edged with black and white.

The Cardiff Railway was one of those local concerns, weaving its way among many other railways, depending upon running powers in switching from one area to another, and its affairs must have been a holy terror to sort out within the confines of the Railway Clearing House. But although it operated largely in the Cardiff docks area and had indeed more than a hundred miles of track in the Dock Estate, it contributed 36 locomotives to the enlarged Great Western in 1923. Its so-called 'main line' was reached by running powers over the Rhymney Railway between Cardiff and Heath Junction, and then it made its way into the narrowest part of the Taff Vale, north of Taff's Well where there were three other railways running side by side: the Rhymney, the Barry, and the Taff Vale itself. The 36 locomotives taken into the GWR in January 1923 were subdivided into a miscellaneous collection of nineteenth-century 0–6–0 tanks and two 0–4–0 saddle tanks specially adapted for working on the sharpest curves and in the most confined spaces in the dock areas. There were also three of the standard GWR saddle tanks, and a 2–4–2 Webb radial tank purchased from the LNWR.

The most important engines, so far as future working was concerned, were three 0–6–2 side tanks designed by Hurry Riches of the Taff Vale, and built by Kitsons in 1908. Curiously enough they were more powerful than anything he designed for the Taff Vale itself, having cylinders 1in larger in diameter than those of the '04' class. These Cardiff Railway 0–6–2 tanks were heavy and powerful units, and lasted a long time under Great Western ownership. Four further 0–6–0

Page 35. (above) *De Glehn compound 'Atlantic' No 104* Alliance *as running in 1920-2;* (centre) The Great Bear, *in Old Oak Common shed;* (below) The Great Bear *on the 10.45am express ex-Paddington, passing Twyford*

Page 36. (above) *5.30am Paddington–Penzance express climbing Rattery Incline, hauled by 2–6–2 tank No 3121 and 4–6–0 No 2922* Saint Gabriel; (below) *'The Torbay Limited' arriving at Kingswear hauled by a '45XX' class 2–6–2 tank*

tank engines were built new for the Cardiff Railway in 1920. They had long saddle tanks extending from cab to the front of the smokebox, and were so long as locomotives that they looked as though they ought to have been 0–6–2s. They too were long-lived engines, and were all rebuilt by the GWR with standard boilers and pannier tanks. In pre-grouping days the locomotives of the Cardiff Railway were painted in a lined-black style resembling that of the London & North Western Railway.

Another Welsh railway contributing the odd three dozen locomotives to GWR stock was the Rhondda & Swansea Bay. This line, beginning with an end-on junction with the Taff Vale at Treherbert, left the Rhondda valley dramatically through the long Rhondda Tunnel and then made its way down to the sea at Port Talbot. From there the line continued parallel with the Great Western main line, and weaving from one side of it to the other, and then after Court Sart, running beside the GWR line to Swansea East Dock. The locomotive stock that had been built specially for the line consisted of 0–6–0 and 0–6–2 side tanks and three smart 2–4–2 tanks; these were all of nineteenth-century vintage, though additions to the stud of 0–6–2 tanks had been made in 1904. Apart from these three classes 0–6–0T, 0–6–2T and 2–4–2T, there was an assortment of secondhand 0–6–0 pannier and saddle tanks obtained from the Great Western at various times. Like the other South Wales engines many of these R & SB examples continued in service after the grouping.

The Cambrian Railways were not in very good shape at the time of grouping, at any rate so far as locomotive power was concerned. The company was using 4–4–0s for passenger, and 0–6–0s for goods and there was very little that could be termed modern. Two of the somewhat exiguous stock of 4–4–0s had been totally destroyed in the Abermule head-on collision in January 1921 and these had been replaced by a couple of the small-wheeled '35XX' class of Great Western 4–4–0. Very soon after grouping the Great Western drafted a considerable number of 2–4–0s to the Cambrian section. The strength of certain bridges and the short length of the turntable at Afonwen precluded the use of any larger engines at first, but the fact that the Cambrian, unlike the other Welsh railways, was

C

quickly furnished with Great Western engines tells its own tale. The passenger locomotive stock included four ancient 2–4–0s, twenty-seven 4–4–0s of nineteenth-century vintage and only four 4–4–0s built as comparatively recently as 1904. There were twenty-nine assorted 0–6–0s, of which the twelve engines of the '89' class had been built at various times between 1903 and 1919. Of the rest there were a few curiosities like the 4–4–0 tank engines purchased from the Metropolitan, two of which were converted into tender engines, and some smart little 0–4–4 tanks. After grouping it was no more than natural that the Cambrian section proper should have been to some extent integrated with the purely Great Western workings on the Ruabon–Dolgelly line.

In pre-grouping days the Cambrian had been perhaps more closely associated with the London & North Western, rather than with the Great Western. Through its connections at Whitchurch and at Shrewsbury there were through carriage services from Aberystwyth to Manchester and to Euston, while all the mail services from Central Wales lines owned by the Cambrian were operated via Crewe. Down the lengthy branch line that followed the Wye valley from Llanidloes to Three Cocks Junction, and to the Brecon & Merthyr Railway at Talyllyn Junction there were occasional services worked by Cambrian engines that penetrated as far south as Merthyr Town. One of these had its post-grouping sequel in a Saturdays-only excursion train from Pennychain Holiday Camp station, near Pwellheli. This made its way down the coast to Dovey Junction, and thence to Moat Lane. Then it proceeded down the Wye Valley line, eventually reached Merthyr and reversed direction, finally clocking into Pontyprid, if the working timetable was to be believed, at 4.33½pm!

Finally, among the principal Welsh constituents I come to the Barry Railway, which in some ways was the most significant of them all. For one thing its locomotive stock, taken in its entirety, was by far the most modern. The railway itself was not incorporated until the year 1884, and its first locomotives were delivered in 1888. The Barry subsequently held the probably unique record of not scrapping a single locomotive in the whole of its existence as an independent company. Between 1888 and 1914 a total of 148 locomotives were purchased, and 148 went into the stock of the GWR on 1 January 1923. But the Barry brought in much more than 148 well-maintained locomotives. All but ten of the locomotive stock were ordered during the time that J. H. Hosgood was locomotive superintendent. He held office from the start of the railway until 1905, and then he was followed, for four years, by H. F. Golding. At the end of 1909 the directors made an appointment of much significance. Both the preceeding locomotive superintendents had been 'Taff' men, but now they brought in a man from outside Wales, 39 years of age, with a wide and varied experience, John Auld. He had served his apprenticeship on the Glasgow & South Western, under that great engineer Hugh Smellie. He subsequently had experience on the Great North of Scotland, under James Johnson, and on the London Tilbury & Southend under Thomas Whitelegg. He then returned to the Glasgow & South Western in the Manson era, to become district locomotive superintendent in Glasgow. He thus brought to the Barry the rich experience of working with some of the most distinguished engineers of the day. It so happened that he was called upon to provide no more than ten new locomotives for the Barry Railway, but his career in the south was barely launched when grouping came, and he entered the service of the Great Western Railway. I need only add at this point that in nine years of grouping he had made his mark to such an extent that he was chosen to succeed Stanier as principal assistant to the chief mechanical engineer, when Stanier went to the LMS in January 1932. He held that high office for nine momentous years.

On the Barry Railway John Auld took charge of a first-rate stud of locomotives. Hosgood had established a high degree of standardisation, using the same type of boiler on a number of different classes, and through being able to purchase most of his locomotives from one manufacturer. No fewer than 95 out of the first 116 locomotives were built by Sharp, Stewart & Co; these engines were as shown in Table 5.

In 1899 the Barry Railway urgently needed more of the standard 0–6–2 tanks. Sharp Stewart were able to take an order for no more than twelve, and so orders for five more were placed with the Cooke Locomotive Works of Paterson,

TABLE 5

Class	Type	No built
A	0–6–0T	5
B, B1	0–6–2T	52*
C	2–4–0T	4†
D	0–8–0	4
F	0–6–0ST	13
G	0–4–4T	2‡
H	0–8–2T	7
J	2–4–2T	8§

*10 built by Vulcan Foundry   †One converted to 2–4–2 type
‡2 built by Hudswell Clarke   §3 built by Hudswell Clarke

The same boiler suited classes A, B, B1, F, G, and J, that is all except the small 2–4–0 tanks and the eight-coupled engines.

New Jersey, and another five from the S.A. Franco-Belge, of Liége. The last mentioned were built to the standard Barry Railway drawings, and were of Class 'B1', but the Americans, in order to give delivery, insisted on giving the nearest they could to the general Barry specification, but using their own standard parts. Thus came Class 'K', with *outside* cylinders. The introduction of the 0–8–0 tender engines came about largely by accident. Sharp Stewart had built some outside-cylindered 0–8–0s with four-wheeled tenders for the then Swedish & Norwegian Railway. This concern found itself unable to pay for them, and Sharp Stewart refused to deliver. The Barry bought two of them in 1889 and another two in 1897. They were not standard, as regards fittings, with other Barry engines; but they were powerful engines and very useful on the coal trains on the Brecon & Merthyr extension line. The Barry, through this piece of luck in acquiring four unwanted engines, became the first British railway to operate 0–8–0 tender engines, beating the London & North Western to it by three years. The 0–8–2 tank engines, a natural development, followed in 1896. These were no accident but were specified by Mr Hosgood. The American 0–6–2 tanks were all fitted with the standard boiler, as used on classes A, B, B1, F, G, and J, in due course; but they were retained, as

40

outside-cylinder engines, well into the grouping era and two of them received Great Western taper boilers.

John Auld's 0–6–4 tank engines of 1914 were built by Hawthorn, Leslie & Co, and were essentially heavy freighters. On the basis of nominal tractive effort they were considerably the most powerful engines on the line. Although their coupled wheels were larger than those of the 0–8–0s and of the 0–8–2 tanks, 4ft 7in against 4ft 3in, the cylinder diameter was 18½in against 18in and the boiler 180lb per square inch against 150. There was an inclination at one time to use some of them on passenger trains, but like other locomotives of this wheel arrangement, such as those of the South Eastern & Chatham, and of the Midland, they were not good riding engines at any speed. In any case they were hardly suited to fast running and coupled wheels as small as 4ft 7in diameter. They were the last new locomotives built for the Barry Railway. After grouping a few of them were fitted with standard Great Western type taper boilers, but the class was withdrawn and scrapped in 1926.

The Barry Railway was not absorbed by the Great Western; it was amalgamated, and ended its individual existence on 1 January 1922, a year before the grouping proper. John Auld was appointed mechanical engineer at Barry Docks and divisional locomotive superintendent for the newly-established Cardiff Valleys Division of the GWR locomotive department; but in September 1922 he was appointed docks assistant to the CME, and in January 1924 docks and personal assistant. He held this office till he succeeded Stanier as principal assistant. Throughout his career on the Great Western Railway he naturally had a special association with the affairs of South Wales, until he had finally amassed a total of nearly fifty-four years in railway service.

CHAPTER 3

Swindon Men

AT the time of the grouping of the railways, in January 1923, the organisation of the locomotive departments of the GWR became unique among the major companies of Great Britain. It became, in fact, the only one where the term 'locomotive department' meant a single organisation. While a few of the pre-grouping companies had followed the Midland precedent of 1907 in relieving the chief mechanical engineer of the responsibility for running staff, on most lines all the running staff, including the footplate men, were on the strength of the locomotive department. At the time of grouping it was natural that the new LMS organisation should follow the Midland pattern, while the Southern followed that of the South Eastern & Chatham. On the latter line the running superintendent was an independent officer, while on the LMS he came under the general superintendent. The LNER followed the SE & CR pattern, except that there were independent running superintendents in each of the three areas, each reporting to the area general manager. On the enlarged Great Western Railway no change was made to the existing organisation, except to set up a new Locomotive, Carriage and Wagon Division for the Welsh lines amalgamated or absorbed.

In 1923, therefore, there were divisional locomotive, carriage and wagon superintendents at Old Oak Common, Bristol, Newton Abbot, Newport, Neath, Cardiff Valleys, Worcester, Wolverhampton and Oswestry. The officers holding these positions enjoyed a high degree of autonomy in their own areas. The more senior, such as those at Newton Abbot and Wolverhampton, both having considerable repair shops as well as running sheds, were like chief mechanical engineers in their own right, dealing with locomotives, carriages, wagons and outdoor machinery. It had been the policy of Churchward to build up a staff of senior men who were all-rounders, who knew all aspects of the chief mechanical engineer's department, both in the divisional organisation, and in the drawing office and works at Swindon headquarters. In the course of promotion men moved from headquarters to divisional posts, from locomotives to carriages and vice-versa. Senior staff were not merely good mechanical engineers, they were good railwaymen, and most important of all good Great Western railwaymen.

In Churchward's day the chief mechanical engineer himself was in a somewhat unique position that stemmed from the original organisation of the GWR in broad gauge times. Churchward, as both Dean and Armstrong before him, was responsible direct to the board of directors. Although several attempts were made to change this and make the CME responsible to the general manager, Churchward successfully fought this off to the end of his career. He regularly attended board meetings, and admitted responsibility only to the chairman of the company. No CME except Webb on the London & North Western had ever held such a position of autonomy. Sir James Inglis had tried to end it in the early nineteen hundreds, and been beaten in the subsequent struggle. Sir Felix Pole tried it again, but Churchward was then on the point of retirement, and the change in the organisational tree was made on the appointment of his successor. But while the old arrangement left the CME very much a king in his own domain it did lead to a certain insularity between the various engineering departments. The fact that each worked through different committees of the board resulted in their tending to work without knowledge, or interest in, what the others were doing. The absence of a strong co-ordinating hand led to some curious anomalies, as will be mentioned later.

To succeed Churchward the board appointed Charles Benjamin Collett, who had been locomotive works manager since 1912. Now Collett was an exception to the general line of promotion of Great Western mechanical engineering officers, having throughout his career been a works man. But in extenuating this departure from normal promotional procedure note must of course be taken of the intervention of the four years of World War I. The Great Western, like other major British railways, undertook numerous tasks of the highest importance in armament production. In view of Collett's exceptional ability as a workshop man one can well understand Churchward's desire to keep him at Swindon, rather than post him to any major divisional appointment that may have fallen vacant at the time. As with Collett himself, the earlier policy began to go more regularly into default in the grouping era, despite the frequent admonitions of Stanier while he was still on the GWR. Until six months before the time of grouping F. G. Wright was chief assistant to the CME. On his retirement Stanier was appointed works assistant to the CME, and shortly afterwards became principal assistant.

The headquarters organisation varied a little from time to time during the remaining twenty-five years of the company. The second-in-command at Swindon was designated principal assistant. Next in the chain of command came the 'outdoor assistant', who was also responsible for locomotive running, and there were separate works managers in charge of the locomotive, and carriage, and wagon works. The post of chief draughtsman was also one of major importance, for it not only carried responsibility for all design work on locomotives, carriages and wagons, but it covered all the locomotive testing work with the dynamometer car and on the stationary testing plant. There was no separate research department in those days. The drawing office was the fountainhead of all technical work in the CME's department. At the time of grouping it must be admitted that the chief draughtsman, G. H. Burrows, was not much more than a titular head of the department. Churchward himself had always enjoyed spending long hours in the drawing office discussing new projects with the individual draughtsmen, and there is no doubt that there were several men who could attribute their subsequent success to 'the Old Man's' personal interest when they were 'on the board'.

In 1925 Burrows was succeeded by F. W. Hawksworth and, with Collett more concerned with works matters than engine and carriage designing, the stature of the chief draughtsman was quickly restored to its earlier eminence. At the same time Stanier, ever mindful of the Churchward tradition of making the experience of the most senior men as broad-based

as possible, had strongly recommended Hawksworth for locomotive works manager when that post fell vacant in 1922.
But Collett, with much very important work in prospect, felt
he could not spare Hawksworth from the drawing office where
he had already been singled out to succeed Burrows, and instead he had put R. A. G. Hannington in. Hannington was
an admirable choice, and left Hawksworth ready for the promotion and in due course to deal with the design of the 'King'
class locomotives. In the meantime Swindon, so far as locomotive practice was concerned, was tending to draw into a
self-exclusive, self-sufficient entity that came to pay less and
less regard to what was going on outside. This was partly due
to the retiring nature of Collett himself, and partly due to the
unhappy aftermath of the Interchange Trials with the LNER
in 1925, which for a time put the Great Western outside the
comity of British locomotive engineering circles.

There was another factor as well. While Collett was a member of both the Institution of Civil and the Institution of
Mechanical Engineers he looked with considerable scepticism
and disfavour upon the Institution of Locomotive Engineers.
Referring no doubt to the admission to membership of men
from the supporting supply industries, the I.Loco.E. was once
described, within the Swindon precints, as 'a lot of b— com-
mercial travellers!' With one exception Great Western men
were not merely discouraged but forbidden to join. The exception was the divisional locomotive, carriage and wagon
superintendent at Old Oak Common, who was instructed to
join and participate to the full, so that Swindon could be
informed as to what was going on in this somewhat suspect
body!

There was a change of attitude in another way too. Churchward took great pride in the fact that when other railways
needed a good man they came to Swindon. He made a
felicitous speech when Pearson was appointed deputy chief
mechanical engineer of the SE & CR in the Maunsell reorgani-
sation of 1913. At that time L. Lynes and H. Holcroft went to
lesser posts at Ashford, entirely with his blessing. Things were
far otherwise with Collett, and although it is carrying the
story to a time ten years after grouping a somewhat revealing
incident may be related. Stanier's departure for the LMS was,

one gathers, not at all to Collett's liking; still less was the obvious incorporation of so many Great Western features in the first LMS Pacific engines of the 'Princess Royal' class. Appropriately, the appearance of these engines was made the subject of a finely illustrated article in *The Railway Gazette*. Not long afterwards Charles S. Lake, then technical editor, had occasion to visit Swindon, and he put his head into a veritable hornet's nest! He was arraigned by Collett in sarcastic terms, for presuming to publish an article of 'x' pages, with 'y' illustrations, as CBC put it: 'all about an engine that *we* designed!' Lake however was an experienced campaigner in the world of technical journalism. He knew Collett's temperament, and was ready with his reply, refuting the impeachment, by reminding him that when the 'Kings' first appeared *The Railway Gazette* carried an even longer and more profusely illustrated article.

In contrast to the somewhat difficult temperament of Collett there was the altogether mellowing influence of Stanier, one of the most popular men who ever held high office at Swindon. He again was a specialist in works matters, but at the same time the very epitome of the Churchward policy of training men to be all-rounders. He was, however, no more than five years junior to Collett in age, and could not have looked forward to succeeding to the chair until relatively late in life. From what I have gathered, both from Stanier himself and those who knew him well, that prospect did not worry him. He was happy and contented in the Swindon atmosphere, and prior to 1931 looked forward to nothing more ambitious. It was the same, on a different level, with Hawksworth. At that stage in Great Western locomotive history there was no more devoted disciple of the Churchward era. Hawksworth had won his spurs in the drawing office under 'the Old Man', and in designing to the broad requirements specified by Collett, or perhaps more subtly by Sir Felix Pole, he followed the precepts of Churchward with no more than the slightest deviation.

As chief draughtsman, Hawksworth was directly responsible for experimental work and dynamometer car testing. The stationary testing plant, known in the works as 'the home trainer', was not then put to any serious use. It was still of its original somewhat limited capacity, and was used occasionally for running locomotives for show purposes on the occasion of organised visits to the works. The dynamometer car, on the other hand, played an important and indeed momentous part in British locomotive history in those first years of grouping. Under the leadership of two senior draughtsmen, E. Pearce and C. K. Dumas, some test results were obtained that shook the locomotive world to its foundations. Pearce and Dumas, by the strict discipline that they applied to all their testing work, laid the foundations for the still more important developments in testing achieved later by Charles Roberts, A. W. J. Dymond and S. O. Ell. But despite the very serious attitude adopted towards their work, Dumas in particular was a great character. There is a cartoon of him in the Swindon archives showing him packing his bag: 'Ready for the "double-home"', as the title went, and into a tattered old Gladstone bag was going nothing but a nightshirt and the maximum number of bottles of beer that could be got into that bag. To be out with him on a 'double-home' was always something of an adventure. He was a widely read and well travelled man, and whatever the hour his young protégés had to be taken round and shown the sights at their staging point, even if it meant, as on one wartime task, shinning up a monument in order to read the inscription by lighted matches in the blackout.

In both the locomotive and the carriage works at Swindon great store was set upon the craftsmanship and know-how of individual men, and the chargehands and fitters in the celebrated 'A' shop—the main locomotive erecting shop—were a remarkably fine body of men. Those were the days when a great deal was left to the shops. Drawings were far less detailed than is now considered necessary and although Collett introduced many improved methods of production there often existed that gap between the information given on the drawing and the finished article, covered by that vague but very significant term 'shop practice'. As recently as 1946 I myself came across an instance that typified this situation. In that year the Westinghouse Brake and Signal Company received a contract to build some vacuum brake cylinders for the Great Western Railway. As chief draughtsman it was my job to act as liaison between Swindon and our own works, and to ensure that we had all the necessary information for manufacture. Going carefully through the Swindon drawings we found a number of points that were obscure, so a meeting with my opposite number on the GWR was arranged, and one by one the various queries were brought up. In nine cases out of ten the Swindon drawing office did not know the answers. We had to go into the works and ask the chargehands. Sometimes even *they* did not know, and the questions were finally resolved by talking to the fitters on the bench. Those cylinders, as turned out at Swindon, were a fine job, but a vast amount of workshop know-how had to be added to the drawings before a works strange to the job could make them.

Throughout the period between the two world wars Great Western locomotive working was maintained at a very high standard. A factor that made a major contribution to this state of affairs was the close liaison between the drawing office and the locomotive running inspectors. Churchward always treated these men in the same way that a railway civil engineer regards his permanent way inspectors. They were the men whose job it was to see that the tools provided were used in the way they were designed to be used. Churchward took the inspectors into his confidence, and all at Swindon were bidden to give close heed to the reports that came in from them. The greatest care was taken in the introduction of new locomotive classes, to ensure that they were driven and fired correctly, and generally speaking the liaison between the running inspectors and the drivers and firemen was cordial. Inevitably there were some inspectors who were less popular than others; but that is merely human nature. At the time of the grouping that outstanding character G. H. Flewellyn was chief locomotive inspector. He was attached to headquarters on the staff of the outdoor assistant to the CME and he was a man of unique experience. In 1904 when working in the Newton Abbot Division he had been chosen by Churchward to supervise the locomotive running on the Ocean Mails during the memorable speed contest with the London & South Western. He was on the *City of Truro* on 9 May 1904 when the record run was made, and ultimately his experience as an inspector extended from days when single-wheelers were still regarded as first line express locomotives to the earliest years of the 'Castles'.

Riding on the footplate was not reckoned to be a dirty job on the GWR. The inspectors wore bowler hats, and few of them wore an overall coat. Firemen were trained to keep their footplates clean, as much as to maintain steam pressure. It was often another matter in my own footplate days, when we had to run with small or indifferent coal; but it is of the 1920s that I am writing now, and old George Flewellyn and his men were able to maintain standards of their own. Flewellyn's son was in the locomotive drawing office at Swindon for many years, thus within one family demonstrating the tightly knit structure of the CME's department. His grandson joined Westinghouse after World War II. I knew him well, and heard from him many stories of his grandfather's remarkable personality.

I have already referred to the autonomy enjoyed by the various divisional locomotive, carriage, and wagon superintendents. It was in many ways reflected in the diversity of ways in which the traffic—and particularly the express passenger traffic—was worked. Although this chapter is titled 'Swindon Men' I am extending it now to Swindon men in a broader sense of the word in that all Great Western locomotive men paid close allegiance to Swindon, whether they were at headquarters or at one of the furthest divisional outposts. To what extent the diversity in locomotive and crew diagramming was due to traditions handed down from tremendous nineteenth-century characters like George Armstrong at Wolverhampton, or whether it was deemed necessary on account of the traffic, I cannot say; but it so happened that Wolverhampton from the early 1920s onward represented one centre where the traditional methods of working had not persisted. Until the opening of the short route to London via Bicester some of the most important London diagrams from Stafford Road depot involved an outward journey via Banbury and return via Worcester. The one-time Paddington–Worcester non-stops were allocated to Stafford Road men, often—and well into the present century—with single-wheelers.

By the early 1920s when I first became familiar with the line to any detailed extent, the Wolverhampton workings had been completely changed. The principal express passenger duties were divided between two links. The first was confined to the London expresses via Bicester, and with the exception of the 9.10am down from Paddington and the 3pm up from Birmingham, the Stafford Road No 1 link had the service to themselves. The most important duties of the No 2 link were northwards to Shrewsbury and Chester, and south-westwards, via Stratford-on-Avon to Bristol. In their restricted sphere of operation both links became very expert, and some of the most experienced observers of the day considered the finest contemporary work anywhere in the British Isles was being done between Paddington and Wolverhampton. It was all the more notable because contrary to the usual run of things on the GWR the locomotives concerned were fired with the local South Staffordshire coal, and not with the choice Welsh grades sometimes quoted as the principal reason for Great Western supremacy in the matter of locomotive performance. But as previously mentioned, whether working 'Stars', 'Saints', 'Counties' or 'Cities', the Stafford Road men of that era were experts and enthusiasts to the last degree.

The working arrangements at Old Oak Common were quite different. It was considered desirable to have available men who knew the road over all the routes radiating from London: to Weymouth, Paignton, Plymouth (both via Bristol and Castle Cary), to Cardiff, Worcester, Gloucester and Wolverhampton. Except in the case of Plymouth to which there were roughly an equal number of double-home turns shared with Laira shed, most trains working into London were hauled by country-based engines from Newton Abbot, Bristol, Landore, Worcester and Gloucester. There were just enough regular London turns on these routes for the men to retain their route knowledge. Another important factor to be recalled was that few if any of the drivers had regular engines. So far as Old Oak Common was concerned, if a driver was working to Plymouth, or Paignton he would almost certainly be allocated a 'Star' and equally so on the 9.10am to Wolverhampton; but elsewhere it could be a dive in the lucky bag, ranging from a 'Flower' or a 'Country' up to *The Great Bear*, if the destination was Swindon.

Such was the far-extended scope and activities of the chief mechanical engineer's department of the GWR, where locomotives were concerned. It also included carriages and wagons, and such historic installations as the pumping machinery for the Severn Tunnel at Sudbrook. Into such an organisation the Welsh constituents were readily fitted, and men from those celebrated little railways came to play an important part in later Great Western developments.

CHAPTER 4

The Standard Two-Cylinder Engine

I T was in 1901, a year before he had succeeded Dean as loco-motive carriage and wagon superintendent, that Churchward had prepared a drawing showing a series of standard locomotive types which he then considered would be able to handle the entire main line traffic of the GWR. In all these the basic 'engine' had two outside cylinders and inside Stephenson link motion. Although the period in which this engine design was developed lies well outside the period of this book, and although the development of the two-cylinder 'engine' was virtually completed a good ten years before grouping, the edifice that Churchward had built up in those momentous first ten years of his chieftainship remained the very corner-stone of Great Western locomotive practice until the end of the separate existence of the company itself. The development of the four-cylinder engines was a collateral but quite distinct and dissimilar activity. A clear understanding of the simple, but vitally important, principles underlying the two-cylinder engine design is essential to an appreciation of Great Western locomotive practice as a whole.

Churchward had been one of the first British engineers to design locomotives expressly for high speed running, and to think beyond the generally accepted standard of 60mph as the hallmark of express speed to be sustained on level track. It is true that in the Race to the North in 1895 locomotives of the London & North Western, Caledonian, and North Eastern Railways had run at 70 to 75mph on level track; but, except perhaps on the Caledonian, such speeds were not de-manded by the ordinary day-to-day express schedules, and the aftermath of the Preston accident in 1896 virtually closed the door upon future Anglo-Scottish acceleration. In the mean-

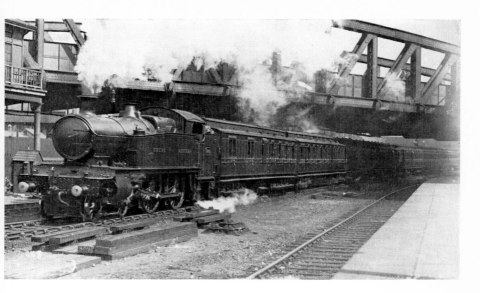

Page 53. (above) *Suburban express train leaving Paddington hauled by a 4–4–2 'County tank' locomotive;* (below) *a '61XX' 2–6–2 tank engine, on Reading–Newbury fast train near Southcote Junction*

Page 54. (above) *A Taff Vale 'U1' class 0–6–2 tank engine No 195 in pre-grouping livery;* (centre) *a Taff Vale 'A' class 0–6–2 tank No 299 as rebuilt with* GWR *boiler;* (below) *ex-Barry Railway: one of the American-built 0–6–2 tanks as rebuilt with* GWR *boiler*

time Churchward's increasing influence in the closing years of the Dean regime at Swindon led to the production of the 'Atbara' class of outside-framed 4–4–0s, and the excellent cylinder and valve design of those engines made them extremely free running. But Churchward's study of contemporary American practice convinced him of the advantages to be derived from outside cylinders, while retaining, as was then standard practice in the USA, the link motion *inside*. While in later years every railway of any consequence in North America changed to one form or another of outside valve gear, Churchward and his successors kept the Great Western valve gear inside.

Many engineers, to whom accessibility of all working parts became something of a religion, were inclined to regard this Great Western practice of using inside valve gear as an archaic survival of a long obsolete practice. Stephenson link motion was in any case regarded by some engineers as an outmoded form of steam distribution. The immense advantage of the link motion in a range of standard locomotives such as Churchward was propounding in 1901 has, however, yet to be discussed. In the earliest stages of the development is was simply a case of inside versus outide valve gear. The question is mainly one of maintenance. In the ordinary way a big-end needs attention more often than the valve gear. If the valve gear is outside it has to be take down, partially at any rate, before one can dismantle the connecting rod to attend to the big-end. There is, therefore, every justification for having the valve gear inside, and this of course was being done on many large British engines of which the Great Central & North Eastern 'Atlantics' and 4–6–0s were examples.

Then Churchward set the yardstick of performance for the new express passenger 4–6–0s at 70mph. On every consideration he set out to secure maximum efficiency of working at that speed: free-running; minimum coal and water consumption, simplicity in management on the footplate. At that period in locomotive history no engineer having anything but the most parochial of outlooks could fail to be impressed by the performance of the du Bousquet-de Glehn four-cylinder compound 4–4–2s on the Northern Railway of France. In my book the *Stars, Castles and Kings of the* GWR I have told in detail how Churchward's interest led to the development of the Swindon series of four-cylinder simple 4–6–0s; but now I am concerned with how this French influence affected the development of the *two*-cylinder engine design. Churchward set out deliberately to produce a simple engine that would have a thermal efficiency as good, if not better, than the French compound, and in one respect he had the advantage of starting second in the race. He was designing something to compete with a French design that was already three or four years old. He settled first the basic proportions of the cylinders. I have in my possession an original letter he wrote to Mr A. V. Goodyear, which is worth quoting. It is dated 25 October 1909. After some references to the four-cylinder engines, and which of them were at that time superheated, the letter continues:

> As you say, the 30in stroke is not a disadvantage as commonly supposed. We have never noticed any abnormal wear and tear with the cylinders and pistons.
>
> It is correct that there are great advantages in the 30in stroke in the matter of expansive working. The long stroke in relation to the bore is the only way we know of making the simple engine equal in efficiency to the compound engine.
>
> You are correct in assuming that the adoption of the 4-cylinder design was not on account of any dissatisfaction with the 18in by 30in cylinders—the relation of stroke to bore is even greater in the 4-cylinders than in the 2-cyls. The 4-cylinder engines are naturally better balanced and have their working parts very much lighter, so making them more suitable for high speed expresses than would be any 2-cylinder engines of equivalent power.
>
> Yours truly
> (signed) G. J. Churchward

All other factors being equal, however, the compound has two inherent advantages. The ratio of expansion in each individual cylinder being less, there is less variation in temperature, and the radiation losses can be more closely controlled and reduced. Secondly, the exhaust beat being much softer, there is a more even draught on the fire, and less tendency to draw fuel unburnt into the exhaust when the engine is working heavily. Both these advantages of compounding have been very thoroughly exploited in recent years by Monsieur Chapelon. But in 1903-5 Churchward was competing against the products of du Bousquet and de Glehn, and the science of internal streamlining, for one thing, was then largely undeveloped. The first de Glehn compounds on the Paris–Orleans Railway had a poor steam distribution, which resulted in the low pressure cylinders not doing anything like their fair share of the work. On the GWR it was a case of a very good compound against a superb simple engine, and the issue was settled for all time so far as the GWR was concerned in favour of the simple. Quite apart from the basic cylinder proportions, and the excellent design of valves and steam passages, two other features of the Churchward two-cylinder simple engines must be specially noted. To aid in securing high thermal efficiency the clearance volume must be a minimum. But while this gave high thermal efficiency it did tend to restrict the power output at high speed. The Churchward two-cylinder express passenger 4–6–0s gave their optimum performance at 55 to 65mph. After that the curve of drawbar horsepower began to fall off fairly rapidly. They certainly attained the target of a 2-ton drawbar horsepower at 70mph, but at lower speeds they were proportionately *puissant* to a far greater degree.

An important characteristic of the Stephenson's link motion is that the 'lead' increases as the engine is linked up. The 'lead' is the amount by which the admission valve is open to steam before the piston reaches the end of its stroke. In high speed running the 'lead' opening is necessary to provide a degree of cushioning on the piston as it approaches the end of its stroke. An advantage frequently claimed for the Walschaerts radial valve gear is that the lead is constant at all cut-offs, and on British express locomotives of large power it was usually made about $\frac{3}{16}$in. For his new express passenger 4–6–0s competing against the French compounds Churchward devised an original and unorthodox setting of the Stephenson link motion. Basing this design upon the fact that 'lead' on the valves was only essential at full express speed he provided $\frac{1}{8}$in *negative* lead in full gear, this changing to $\frac{1}{8}$in positive lead at normal running cut-off which was around 18 per cent. No cushioning effect was needed when the engine was running slowly, or slogging hard up a heavy bank, and at high speed, 70 to 75mph, there was just the right amount of lead to provide for smooth running.

The Standard Two-Cylinder Engine

The 4–6–0 express locomotives were designed to give their optimum performance at 70mph, at which speed Churchward expected a drawbar pull of at least 2 tons to be sustained on level track. The locomotives more than fulfilled this expectation. With the same design of cylinders and valve gear one would expect the standard locomotives with 5ft 8in wheels to develop their optimum performance at about 60mph and those with 4ft 7in wheels at a little under 50mph. Maximum speed performance apart, however, the Swindon setting of the Stephenson link motion on the new standard engines was of outstanding importance in another respect. The four events in the steam cycle taking place in the cylinder of a locomotive —admission, cut-off, release and compression—are interrelated with valves of the conventional slide or piston type, and the point of compression is directly associated with the point of admission. Without going too deeply into technicalities, the later the admission takes place, the later also is the point of compression, and so with no lead, or negative lead, the point of compression is much later than with a locomotive having a constant lead (with Walschaerts gear) of about $\frac{3}{16}$in. There is thus a considerable difference in the cylinder conditions between those of a 'Star' and a 'Saint' when both are slogging uphill, or a cut-off of, say, 35 to 40 per cent. The point of compression would be much earlier on the 'Star', and this feature has the effect of reducing the amount of work done in the cylinder.

This theoretical point has been fully borne out in countless instances of hard work uphill. Both in my own experience and that of other observers, when both types are being well extended uphill, at speeds of around 30mph a 'Saint' was vastly superior to a 'Star'—in fact some of the finest 'Saint' hill-climbing performances eclipse the best recorded 'Castle' runs over the same route. On the other hand there was no question of the superiority of the 'Stars' over the 'Saints' in long-distance high speed running. They had the advantage of being easier on the track, they rode more comfortably, and they did their work on a lighter consumption of coal. A very good measure of the extent to which a locomotive is being opened out is to relate the actual drawbar pull that is being sustained to the nominal tractive effort. A few outstanding performances by 'Saint' class engines are analysed thus in Table 6. These include some medium-speed hard uphill efforts, and relate to the west to north route, via the Severn Tunnel, and to climbs out of the Severn Tunnel with heavy Paddington–South Wales expresses, and runs on the South Wales main line.

Among these runs that of No 2949 *Stanford Court* on the northbound climb to Llanvihangel seems exceptional, for above Abergavenny, with a gross trailing load of 450 tons the speed fell first of all to a sustained 29mph on 1 in 82, and then recovered to 31mph on the subsequent 1 in 95. The best I have ever done with a 'Castle' anywhere on this route was a sustained 34mph with 445 tons on 1 in 100. Although this gave a slightly higher equivalent drawbar horsepower, the 'Castle' had a nominal tractive effort nearly 30 per cent greater than that of the 'Saint'. Moreover that 'Castle' effort was in my experience quite exceptional. With loads of that order the sustained climbing speeds on 1 in 100 gradients were usually less than 30mph. The 'Saints' also had the reputation of being very free-running engines and the first instance Cecil J. Allen ever had of a sustained maximum speed of 90 mph was with No 2915 *Saint Bartholomew* with an up Birmingham express descending the Gerrards Cross bank. Unlike the 'Stars' they were generally driven with a partially opened regulator, and cut–off about 22 or 25 per cent. Worked thus they ran easily up to about 80mph on favourable stretches, though there is always the exception that proves the rule! This was a footplate experience of my own on No 2934 *Butleigh Court*, when the engine was pulled up to 18 per cent with a wide though not full open regulator, and ran freely up to 77mph on level track east of Reading with a 375-ton train.

A remarkable experience of my own, recorded from the train rather than the footplate, was on the first portion of the 2.10pm down Birmingham express at a holiday weekend, when a gross trailing load of 320 tons was worked by No 2906 *Lady of Lynn*. On the level and slightly rising stretch from Northolt to Denham, speed was worked up to 70mph; then the 1 in 175 section to Gerrards Cross bank was taken at a minimum speed of 63½mph while on the subsequent 1 in 264 gradient to Beaconsfield the speed accelerated to a sustained

64½mph. This involved an output of 1,160 equivalent horse-power, and a sustained drawbar pull of 3 tons. This was roughly 28 per cent of the nominal tractive effort of the loco-motive—a very high proportion at such a speed as 64mph. Some further examples of high power-output, including a number at speeds of 60 to 70mph mostly by Landore men on the South Wales expresses, are shown in Table 6.

TABLE 6

PERFORMANCE OF 'SAINT' CLASS LOCOMOTIVES

Engine No	Load tons	Gradient 1 in	Speed mph	DHP	DB Pull tons	Pull — % TE
2901	385	300	56	1000	3	27.8
2906	320	264	64½	1160	3	27.8
2908	380	300	57	1020	3	27.8
2928	420	100	31	1135	6.1	56
2936	345	660	69	924	2.25	20.7
2942	485	660	61	1040	2.85	26
2942	485	300	55½	1220	3.7	34
2949	450	95	31	1270	6.8	62.5
2986	420	300	49	905	3.1	28.4
2986	380	300	57	930	2.3	21

Engine names (relating to the foregoing table):

2901	*Lady Superior*	2936	*Cefntilla Court*
2906	*Lady of Lynn*	2942	*Fawley Court*
2908	*Lady of Quality*	2949	*Stanford Court*
2928	*Saint Sebastian*	2986	*Robin Hood*

I had a number of footplate journeys on them, and from the 'feel' of their going one gained the impression they were at their best at about 55 to 65mph. But there was always a cer-tain amount of vibration off the motion which one never ex-perienced with the four-cylinder 'Stars'. Vibration or not, however, they were universal favourites with the men. During the investigations of the Bridge Stress Committee in 1924-5 they were shown to have a somewhat severe effect on the track, though even the 'Stars' did not emerge from that investigation with the best of reputations. Those trials ended for all time the generally held view of civil engineers that it was the dead weight on the axles that was the principal and in fact the only criterion of the effort a locomotive had on the track, or over-line bridge structures. The balancing arrangements of both 'Saints' and 'Stars' was modified in the light of the test results. The principal dimensions of the 'Saints' as running at the time of grouping are shown in Table 7.

TABLE 7

'SAINT' CLASS LOCOMOTIVES

Cyclinders:

diameter	18½in
stroke	30in

Motion:

Piston valve diameter	10in
Max valve travel	6¼in
Steam lap	1⅝in
Exhaust clearance	NIL
Lead in full fore gear	–0.15in
Cut-off in full gear	77.5%

Tractive effort:

At 85% working pressure	24,395lb

The 'Saints', although the most prominent of the standard two-cylinder locomotives, were only one class, and the same performance characteristics were to be seen in the 'County' class 4–4–0s, and the '43XX' class 2–6–0s. The cylinders were the same on all three classes, but it is clear that the smaller boilers of the eight-wheeled locomotives could not supply those cylinders to provide comparable power outputs. Furthermore, the No 4 boilers carried a pressure of only 200lb per square inch. Transitorily, however, both classes were capable of a very high output of power for their size. On the west to north route, prior to the introduction of the 4–6–0 engines, some truly splendid work was done by the 'Counties'. I have referred to the 'feel' of the 'Saints' at speed. The 'Counties' were generally rough-riding engines. It was not a dangerous roll or pitch, but a generally rough action. But they were such willing and reliable engines in other respects that the crews just set their teeth, and let them run. I shall always remember an occasion, long after all the 4–4–0 'Counties' had been scrapped when Chief Locomotive Inspector Andress called at my home in Bath, and there was time to run a few trains on my 0-gauge model railway. I then had three Hornby 4–4–0s, an LNER 'Hunt', a Midland compound, and the GWR No 3821 *County of Bedford*. They all had the same chassis and could have expected to be identical in their action. The 'Hunt' and the compound were most staid and circumspect runners; but the 'County' was a wild thing, and immensely strong. Bill Andress watched her go round several times and then remarked: 'Rough as the devil; just like she always was!'

The 2–6–0s were splendid mixed traffic locomotives. The valve setting which made the 'Saints' so strong on the banks gave to all the two-cylinder classes a massive capacity for rapid acceleration. This was used to great advantage by the stud of 2–6–0s stationed in Cornwall. There the main line abounds in steeply-graded starts from intermediate stops, and the 2–6–0s used to get clearly away and mount the banks in most efficient style. At the time of grouping the Cornish Riviera Express used to run non-stop between Plymouth and Truro in each direction. The normal load was one of five 70ft coaches for Penzance, with one through carriage each for St Ives and Falmouth. A Penzance 'Mogul' used to run the train down from Plymouth to Truro, then this engine would come off, and be replaced by another 'Mogul' with the first engine continuing to Penzance with the all-stations local that followed from Truro. I remember this procedure well, because day return excursion tickets between Cornish stations were not available on the Cornish Riviera Express. The 'Moguls' were not taxed by the normal summer workings in Cornwall. They were highly appreciated by all concerned, and I remember being shown the coal sheets for the engines stationed at Penzance, and noting there was not an engine of the class that was the using more than 35lb of coal per mile—all in.

They were much smoother and more comfortable riding than the 'Counties'. This is no relative expression; they were like little Rolls–Royces when nicely tuned up. My own footplate experience of them came many years later on the Llangollen–Barmouth line, and there on a heavily-graded, sharply-curved route they were most enjoyable engines to ride. Vehicle-wise, of course, there was all the difference in the world between a 2–6–0, with drive on the middle pair of coupled wheels, and a high-stepping 4–4–0 with drive on the leading pair. While the 'Counties' appeared capable of very high output of power, transitorily the 'Moguls' seemed able to sustain such outputs for an almost unbelievable length of time; and this leads me to mention an astonishing performance that I once recorded with engine No 5346. The series of fast express trains from Birmingham Snow Hill to Paddington included some that made two intermediate stops, and were allowed 2hr 5min overall. One of these was the 6.0pm up, but that train was unusual in that it included two separate London portions, one going direct via Bicester, and the other going via Oxford. It was always a heavy train out of Birmingham, and it was unusual in another respect that the engine working it from Wolverhampton came off at Leamington and took the Oxford portion, while a fresh London engine took the Bicester line portion.

In the 1920s my own opportunities for travel were necessarily confined to weekends and holiday times, and while this sometimes led to my experiencing unpunctual running it had the advantage of often producing loads much above the normal. So it certainly was with this run on the 6.0pm up, which on this occasion I joined as far north as Chester. The Mogul No 5346 was our engine from Shrewsbury, and with a load of 380 tons she had no difficulty in keeping the sectional times to Wolverhampton. There, to my surprise, she continued at the head of the train, and with an additional coach added kept time to Birmingham. There, however, *two more* coaches were added, bringing the gross trailing load up to 470 tons, for the first leg of an up 2hr Birmingham express! The immense potentialities of the Churchward two-cylinder 'engine' aided by his magnificent taper boiler were never shown better than in the ensuing run to Leamington. On the gradual rise from Tyseley out to Knowle on which speed gradually rose to $60\frac{1}{2}$ mph, I calculate that this little engine was 700 equivalent drawbar horsepower, or 18 per cent of the nominal tractive effort. The log of this remarkable performance is shown in

Table 8, and it will be seen that the finely sustained uphill effort from Tyseley was capped by a maximum speed of 75mph down Hatton bank.

TABLE 8

GWR BIRMINGHAM–LEAMINGTON

Load: 434 tons tare 470 tons full
Engine: 2–6–0 No 5346

Distance Miles		Actual min sec		Speeds mph
0.0	BIRMINGHAM	0	00	—
1.1	Bordseley	3	15	—
3.2	Tyseley	6	05	51
7.0	Solihull	10	35	48
8.5	Widney Manor	12	20	56½
10.4	Knowle	14	15	60½
12.9	Lapworth	16	40	69
17.1	Hatton	20	35	60
21.3	Warwick	24	15	75
23.3	LEAMINGTON	26	25	—

At a time when the London suburban services were worked mainly by the 4–4–2 'County' tanks and by the little Armstrong 2–4–0s, some of the heavier Birmingham commuter services were in the hands of the '31XX' 2–6–2 tanks. Mr A. V. Goodyear, to whom posterity is indebted for such a wealth of Great Western running data over a period of more than fifty years, did not neglect to notice the work done on his daily business trains between Solihull and Birmingham, and these provide further highly convincing evidence of the efficacy of the Churchward valve setting for producing vigorous acceleration from rest.

Last among this distinguished two-cylinder family were the 2–8–0s. I never had an opportunity of riding on one of them, but two quite dissimilar incidents must be related. The first took place in the last year before grouping, and in Scotland above all places. William Whitelaw was then chairman of the North British Railway, and the time had come when the freight traffic of that company was needing something more powerful than the excellent Reid superheated 0–6–0s, that eventually became LNER class 'J36'. Whitelaw was a great believer in locomotive interchange trials. It had been due to him that one of the Reid 'intermediate' class of 4–4–0—the non-superheated predecessors of the famous 'Glen'—had been tested against a Highland 'Castle' class 4–6–0, and also that a North British 'Atlantic' had made some experimental runs between Carlisle and Preston against an LNWR 'Experiment' 4–6–0. Similarly, in 1921 it was at his instigation that some test runs were made with heavy freight trains on the Glenfarg Bank—on the Perth–Edinburgh line—between a North Eastern three-cylinder 0–8–0 of class 'T3', and a Great Western '28XX' 2–8–0. The respective performances were measured in the North Eastern dynamometer car. There is no doubt that in this particular set of trials the Great Western engine came off second best so far as actual hauling power was concerned. How the technical results compared I do not know. but in this affair the Swindon engine and its men were up against a most formidable competitor in J. J. Weatherburn, the dynamometer car inspector of the NER.

Many years later, when he had retired, I had the pleasure of visiting him at his home at Rowlands Gill, and he recalled with the utmost relish how he had 'outwitted' the GWR men. The tests were made up the formidable 1 in 75 ascent from Bridge of Earn to Glenfarg, up a stretch of line very much exposed to the weather, and then when shelter is obtained in rock cuttings the overhanging trees can also be something of a menace. Weatherburn contrived it that the Great Western 'batted' first. The weather was bad and on one trip, the '28XX' slipped to a standstill. Her 'dry' sanding gear was not a great deal of help in the strong cross-wind that brought snow with it. Then Weatherburn made one run, very much with his tongue in his cheek, taking the same load as the GWR engine but at a slightly slower speed. Then the '28XX' made another run, her best in the series. But the North Eastern men, having taken the measure of the opposition, asked for a considerably heavier load, threw in all they had, and made the fastest climb of the whole series. The honours were with Darlington.

The 'sign audible' of the Churchward setting of the Stephenson link motion on all the standard engines was the truly explosive bark of the exhaust when starting away, and I had some experience of that exhaust when I was engaged on design work for resignalling at Cardiff in the 1930s. We built some lengthy signal bridges carrying colour light signals relating to many running lines, and after they were in place we were requested to add smokeplates of timber to protect the steel gantries from the direct blast of locomotive exhausts. These plates extended about 3ft on either side of the steelwork, and then complaints began to come in of the signal lights occasionally going out. What was actually happening was that the exhausts of the '28XX' engines blasting their way through with heavy coal trains were striking the outermost ends of the smokeplates with such force as to twist the whole gantry. The colour light signals having a concentrated beam of light were tilted upwards when the gantry structure twisted, and it appeared from rail level as though the lights had momentarily gone out. Some strengthening of the structure had to be made to resist this strong twisting effect.

Incidentals apart, the Great Western Railway entered the grouping era with the stud of standard two-cylinder locomotives forming a magnificent tool of operation. How that tool was developed in later years can be appropriately concluded with a list of the named express passenger engines of the 'Saint' and 'County' classes, thus:

Original Churchward experimental engines—

2900   *William Dean* (originally No 100)
2998   *Ernest Cunard* (originally No 98)
2971   *Albion* (originally No 171)

First standard ten-wheelers—

2972	*The Abbot*	2976	*Winterstoke*
2973	*Robin Bolitho*	2977	*Robertson*
2974	*Lord Barrymore*	2978	*Kirkland*
2975	*Sir Ernest Palmer*	2979	*Quentin Durward*
	(originally	2980	*Coeur de Lion*
	Viscount Churchill)	2981	*Ivanhoe*

2982	*Lalla Rookh*	2987	*Bride of Lammermoor*
2983	*Redgauntlet*	2988	*Rob Roy*
2984	*Guy Mannering*	2989	*Talisman*
2985	*Peveril of the Peak*	2990	*Waverley*
2986	*Robin Hood*		

The later '29XX' series—

2901	*Lady Superior*	2929	*Saint Stephen*
2902	*Lady of the Lake*	2930	*Saint Vincent*
2903	*Lady of Lyons*	2931	*Arlington Court*
2904	*Lady Godiva*	2932	*Ashton Court*
2905	*Lady Macbeth*	2933	*Bibury Court*
2906	*Lady of Lynn*	2934	*Butleigh Court*
2907	*Lady of Provence*	2935	*Caynham Court*
2908	*Lady of Quality*	2936	*Cefntilla Court*
2909	*Lady Disdain*	2937	*Clevedon Court*
2910	*Lady of Shalott*	2938	*Corsham Court*
2911	*Saint Agatha*	2939	*Croome Court*
2912	*Saint Ambrose*	2940	*Dorney Court*
2913	*Saint Andrew*	2941	*Easton Court*
2914	*Saint Augustine*	2942	*Fawley Court*
2915	*Saint Bartholomew*	2943	*Hampton Court*
2916	*Saint Benedict*	2944	*Highnam Court*
2917	*Saint Bernard*	2945	*Hillingdon Court*
2918	*Saint Catherine*	2946	*Langford Court*
2919	*Saint Cuthbert*	2947	*Madresfield Court*
2920	*Saint David*	2948	*Stackpole Court*
2921	*Saint Dunstan*	2949	*Stanford Court*
2922	*Saint Gabriel*	2950	*Taplow Court*
2923	*Saint George*	2951	*Tawstock Court*
2924	*Saint Helena*	2952	*Twineham Court*
2925	*Saint Martin*	2953	*Titley Court*
2926	*Saint Nicholas*	2954	*Tockenham Court*
2927	*Saint Patrick*	2955	*Tortworth Court*
2928	*Saint Sebastian*		

The 'County' class 4–4–0s—

3800	*County of Middlesex*	3802	*County Clare*
3801	*County Carlow*	3803	*County Cork*

3804	*County Dublin*	3822	*County of Brecon*
3805	*County Kerry*	3823	*County of Carnarvon*
3806	*County Kildare*	3824	*County of Cornwall*
3807	*County Kilkenny*	3825	*County of Denbigh*
3808	*County Limerick*	3826	*County of Flint*
3809	*County Wexford*	3827	*County of Gloucester*
3810	*County Wicklow*	3828	*County of Hereford*
3811	*County of Bucks*	3829	*County of Merioneth*
3812	*County of Cardigan*	3830	*County of Oxford*
3813	*County of Carmarthen*	3831	*County of Berks*
3814	*County of Chester*	3832	*County of Wilts*
3815	*County of Hants*	3833	*County of Dorset*
3816	*County of Leicester*	3834	*County of Somerset*
3817	*County of Monmouth*	3835	*County of Devon*
3818	*County of Radnor*	3836	*County of Warwick*
3819	*County of Salop*	3837	*County of Stafford*
3820	*County of Worcester*	3838	*County of Glamorgan*
3821	*County of Bedford*	3839	*County of Pembroke*

Two points may be added in respect of the above names. The 'Saint' No 2943 *Hampton Court* was named after the lesser-known stately home near Dinmore, in Herefordshire, and not the famous Royal residence on the Thames. I have often wondered why one of the 'Saints' was not named *Saint Christopher*, for he, after all, was the patron saint of travellers! Ten of the 'Counties' had Irish names, in recognition of the strong associations with the Fishguard–Rosslare service, and the efforts being made to develop the tourist traffic via this route. The naming of the 'Counties' may puzzle some present-day readers. The order of construction was 3800, 3831-3839, 3801-3820, 3821–3830. All except Nos 3821-3830, which were built in 1911-12, had the square front-end framing, as used on the earlier two-cylinder 4–6–0s.

CHAPTER 5

Four-Cylinder 4-6-os

I N *The Stars, Castles and Kings of the GWR* I have told in very full detail the origin and subsequent history of this most famous family of British steam locomotives. In the present book that story must be looked at in the context of Great Western locomotive history as a whole, with the strength and some weaknesses of the four-cylinder stud compared and contrasted with some other famous products of Swindon. At this distance in time the student of locomotive history may well ask why Churchward should have branched out into his four-cylinder development. He had achieved an outstanding success with his two-cylinder engine. He had obtained a higher thermal efficiency than that of the French compound with an incomparably simpler machine, so why depart from this into the greater complication and cost of four-cylinders? Although he was far more inclined to take notice of what was currently happening on other railways than the majority of his English contemporaries he is unlikely to have been influenced by them. On most railways that were then building large ten-wheeled locomotives for express passenger work, notably the Great Central, North Eastern, Great Northern, and Glasgow & South Western, two outside cylinders and inside Stephenson link motion was favoured. It was only the freakish four-cylindered engines of Dugald Drummond on the London & South Western and the inside-cylindered Caledonian 4–6–0s that stood notably apart. In American practice, of which Churchward was a close student, two outside cylinders was the general rule. Even where compounding was favoured, the Vauclain and the tandem systems enabled all the cylinders to be kept outside. On the continent of Europe, however, the reverse prevailed. In addition to that of de Glehn there were

compound systems by Maffei and Gölsdorf that involved inside as well as outside cylinders; and if Churchward had not
been impressed by compounding as such on the de Glehn
'Atlantics' purchased by the GWR he was certainly impressed
by the smooth riding and fine mechanical construction of
these engines.

Now while I would not presume to know, or even to guess,
what was in Churchward's mind at that very interesting and
critical point in his career, it has always seemed to me that in
the years 1906-8 he was thinking in terms of far larger locomotives than his standard two-cylinder 4–6–0s. While he had
comfortably attained with those engines his target of a drawbar pull of 2 tons at 70mph, that 2 tons did not then provide
all that much in the way of hauling capacity where the running characteristics of contemporary Great Western main line
coaching stock was concerned. His development of the famous
70ft stock was barely under way, and the bulk of Great Western trains were composed of the Dean clerestory-roofed stock.
This latter seemed to have an unusually high rolling resistance. A dynamometer car test run on the up Torquay Diner
with one of the 'Knight' series of 4–6–0s showed that a drawbar pull of 2 tons was necessary at 70mph on the level with a
load of no more than 378 tons tare. Modern stock of equal
tonnage would not have involved a drawbar pull of more than
$1\frac{1}{2}$ tons at the same speed. Like the far-sighted all-round railwayman that he was, Churchward foresaw that at the rate
passenger traffic was developing on the line his engines would
before long be called upon to pull far heavier loads.

In view of what was being done on the Northern Railway
of France at that time one is curious to know exactly what the
GWR got out of the de Glehn compounds. In 1906, speaking
at a meeting of the Institution of Mechanical Engineers,
Churchward said that *La France* was one of the few Great
Western engines that could provide a drawbar pull of 2 tons
at 70mph. When some eighteen years ago I was writing my
book *50 Years of Western Express Running* I was privileged
to study the dynamometer car records going back to the early
Churchward days, but strange though it may seem no full-
dress trial of *La France* ever seems to have been made. In my
search I had the help of that enthusiast of enthusiasts for all

Page 71. (above) *Ex-Barry Railway 0–6–4 tank No 1349 rebuilt with* GWR *type boiler;* (centre) *ex-Brecon & Merthyr 0–6–2 tank No 11 as rebuilt;* (below) *the first of the new standard 0–6–2 tanks of the '56XX' class*

Page 72. (above) *Up South Wales express near Reading hauled by No 2949* Stanford Court; (below) *Up Weymouth express passing Reading West: engine No 5971* Merevale Hall

test data, S. O. Ell, who was then in charge of all experimental work, but we found absolutely nothing. At the same time it is hard to believe that no trials were actually made. It is well known that Churchward sometimes took only the most perfunctory interest in the lengthy charts produced in the dynamometer car. They would be laid out in the drawing office for his examination, and the 'Old Man' would come in, put his pocket rule on certain sections, and then stride away. He was no respecter of records, or relics once they had fulfilled their function—as sadly enough we know with the scrapping of the broad-gauge 4–2–2 *Lord of the Isles*, because it was taking up valuable space in the works. It could well be that the rolls relating to tests of *La France* were scrapped because they were short of filing space! But from whatever reason, it seems now that we shall never know by what quantitative amounts the Swindon two-cylinder engines 'had an edge' on *La France*.

All the same *La France* left her mark on Great Western locomotive practice. We know that Churchward was very impressed with her smooth riding and the beautiful workmanship put into her rods and motion work; and the division of the drive suited what could well have been his thoughts towards much larger engines. The first four-cylinder 4–6–0s, with cylinders $14\frac{1}{4}$in diameter by 26in stroke, had a nominal tractive effort almost exactly the same as that of the 'Saints' and there was the opportunity of comparing otherwise identical two-cylinder and four-cylinder locomotives on the same work. In early days of the shortened main line to the West of England 'Saints' and 'Stars' were used indiscriminately on the principal expresses. The four-cylinder engine layout was being proved. In the meantime there took place the remarkable incident of *The Great Bear*. Churchward said publicly that in his view the principal locomotive problem was that of the boiler. If indeed he was thinking in terms of much larger engines what would have been more natural than to build an experimental locomotive with a very much larger boiler than anything built hitherto. The 'engine' layout he had applied to the first 'Stars' was capable of considerable enlargement, and if a locomotive of much greater power was to be built there would be every advantage in having the drive divided between two axles to reduce the loading on the driving axleboxes.

Then there was the question of the valve gear. With the relatively small cylinders fitted to the original 'Stars' it might just have been possible to get Stephenson link motion inside. But what was then possible would have been out of the question when the design was enlarged to the size of the 'Castles' and 'Kings'; and although we do not know if Churchward ever contemplated a locomotive as big as the last-named class his thoughts of bigger engines in the future may well have decided him to abandon the link motion in his four-cylinder engines. Although the 'Stars' did not have the tremendous 'punch' of the two-cylinder engines when starting away and in climbing heavy gradients, the running inspectors reported very favourably on the four-cylinder engines when sustaining high speeds, and in consequence it became the policy to draft them on to the long non-stop runs, such as Paddington–Exeter, Paddington–Plymouth, and Paddington–Newport. In the meantime the establishment of the 70ft coaches as standard on those same express services brought a reduction in the rolling resistance of the trains, and although the dead loads increased, as Churchward had foreseen, the four-cylinder 4–6–0s as originally designed were able to cope satisfactorily. The excellent performance of the No 1 standard boilers, however, enabled the cylinder diameter to be increased to 15in in the later batches of 'Stars', so that the tractive effort at 85 per cent boiler pressure became 27,800lb against the 24,370lb of the 'Saints'. It is an interesting speculation as to whether Churchward if faced with the need for much larger engines in the 1920s would have built them as 'Pacifics', in view of his earlier flirtation with *The Great Bear*.

The 'Stars' were lovely engines. In later years I enjoyed many runs on their footplates, and found, as I had always previously been given to understand, that they responded most impressively when handled on a light rein. For reasons already discussed in the previous chapter they were not so vigorous in getting away as a 'Saint', but with the reverser in 17 to 20 per cent cut-off and the regulator about three-quarters full open there was little they would not do once they had topped about 45mph. They were immense favourites with the men on both sides of the footplate, and with good maintenance the standard of reliability was very high.

Engineers on other railways strongly criticised the inside Walschaerts valve gear, which was certainly inaccessible. However, Great Western locomotive men of all grades had grown up to live with that valve gear, and in all the years I travelled on the line and came to know literally hundreds of the enginemen I never once heard that gear criticised, and never once —even during the worst days of World War II—did I experience a mechanical failure of one of these engines. Some of the finest runs I experienced with the 'Stars' were in the 1920s, when there were still no more than a few 'Castles' and 'Kings' in service; but as I have discussed most of these in detail in *Stars, Castles and Kings of the* GWR, I will just summarise a few of the details in this book, later in Chapter 10.

TABLE 9

STANDARD BOILERS AND RATIOS

Engine Class	'Star'	'4700'	'Castle'	'King'
Heating surfaces sq ft				
Tubes	1686.6	2062.4	1854.3	2007.5
Firebox	154.8	169.8	163.8	193.5
Superheater	262.6	287.5	262.6	313
Total	2104	2519.7	2280.7	2514
Grate area sq ft	27.07	30.28	29.4	34.3
Nominal TE				
Total HS	1.32	1.26*	1.39	1.60†
Grate area	1025	1050 *	1080	1175 †

*Related to 'Castle' tractive effort
†Related to higher boiler pressure, ratios become 1.44 and 1̄025

A study of the important ratios in the dimensions of the three four-cylinder 4–6–0 classes in Table 9 shows clearly the extent to which the 'Castles' were a compromise. It was originally the intention to use the enlarged '47XX' boiler on the 'Castles' and I have included in the tabular summary details of what the respective ratios would have been had this been used with a four-cylinder 'engine' of 'Castle' proportions. It will be seen that the various ratios were approximately the same as those of the 'Stars', and that a perfectly logical enlargement would have resulted. But the weight came out too heavy, and a compromise design of boiler had to be made for the 'Castle'. As it turned out it was very successful, but the restrictions in weight to which the Swindon drawing office had to work could have been a serious handicap. This situation, which seems to have been accepted as just one of those things was, I think, typical of the changed outlook of the chief mechanical engineer's department since Collett succeeded Churchward. Collett, unlike all his predecessors at Swindon, was serving under the rule of a very strong general manager, who had no intention of allowing the locomotive department to continue in the state of autonomy that it had possessed for so long. And Collett, though an extremely able engineer, had to watch his step so far as relations with other departments were concerned. Consequently while it might have crossed his mind, the extent and likely duration of the prevalent weight restrictions on important main lines had probably not concerned him to the point of raising the matter with the civil engineer. Those restrictions were accepted as a perameter within which his department had got to work.

How different it might have been had Churchward still remained in office can be imagined from the incident, some seventeen years earlier, when the proposal to introduce 70ft bogie coaches was launched. What would have amounted to a veto came from the signal engineer of the day, who stated that the proposed new coaches would overspan his facing lock-bars, and so permit of a momentary release of the lock during the passage of one of those coaches. Churchward thereupon had counted up, by his own staff, the total number of lock-bars that would be passed over on the routes where he proposed to run 70ft coaches, and worked out the total cost of lengthening all these lock-bars. When the project of 70ft coaches was raised a second time and the signal engineer made his official objection, Churchward astonished the gathering by showing not only that he knew exactly how many lock-bars would be concerned, but that he had worked out the cost of altering them. The cost was really very small in relation to the great advantages that would be derived from running trains composed of 70ft coaches. Accordingly the signal engineer received instructions to make the necessary alterations and Churchward was authorised to build 70ft coaches.

In the early 1920s had Churchward remained in the chair at Swindon, and he had felt that larger express passenger engines were necessary, one can well imagine that with his keen overall interest in the railway he would have taken care to find out the number of underline bridges that were imposing the prevailing weight restrictions. If he had not been able to find out directly he would have done so indirectly, as he had done in the case of the facing point lock-bars. He would then have discovered how near matters were to clearing the entire line from Paddington to Plymouth via Westbury, for a 22-ton axle-load. As it was that situation leaked out almost by accident. In 1924 *The Great Bear* needed a new boiler. Quite logically it would not have been an economic proposition to build one. The famous engine was severely restricted in her sphere of operation. She was a difficult engine to fit into any normal links, and so Collett decided not to renew the boiler, but to cut down the frames and renew the engine as a 'Castle'. It was a perfectly reasonable step to take, but when the powers that be at Paddington heard that *The Great Bear* had been scrapped they were aghast. She had something of a prestige symbol: the first British 'Pacific', and Collett had some very pointed questions to answer. It was then, and only then, that the weight restrictions imposed by the civil engineer and the reasons for them were brought into the open. Then Sir Felix Pole took a firm hand, and instructed the civil engineer to get the remaining bridges strengthened without delay, and Collett to design a new express passenger locomotive of maximum tractive capacity from an axle load of $22\frac{1}{2}$ tons.

The 'King' class, unhampered by weight restrictions, was much more nearly a true enlargement of the 'Star', except in the mechanical design of the bogie. One of Churchward's fads, if one may presume to call one of the precepts of a great engineer a 'fad', was his insistence on the cylinder centre lines being horizontal and this led the drawing office into difficulties with the large inside cylinders of the 'Kings'. The draughtsman concerned was the late A. W. J. Dymond, and he hit upon the idea of having outside bearings for the leading pair of wheels of the bogie, and inside bearings for the trailing pair. Somewhat hesitatingly he put the idea forward, and to his surprise it was accepted at once. At first there was some trouble with the riding of this bogie, and an alarming derailment occurred with engine No 6004 at over 60mph with the down Cornish Riviera Express near Midgham. Fortunately this took place on a stretch of plain line. Nothing more than the engine bogie was derailed and the driver was able to stop the train in safety. The fine record of the GWR in immunity from accident is frequently commented upon; but no less remarkable is the way in which serious mishaps did occur. The derailment of the bogie of engine No 6004 near Midgham was a case in point. Had there been a crossover in the path of the train, nothing short of a serious wreck could surely have been avoided. A change in the springing eliminated the defects in the riding and the 'Kings' thereafter became among the smoothest and most comfortable riding locomotives to run the rails in Great Britain.

Rarely has a new locomotive type taken the road with more publicity than that given to the 'Kings'. Sir Felix Pole saw to that. The pioneer engine No 6000 *King George V* was placed on exhibition at various centres in aid of the GWR 'Helping Hand Fund', from which employees, or retired employees in need, were helped. Then the engine was shipped to the USA to represent the GWR and Great Britain, at the centenary celebrations of the Baltimore & Ohio Railway. It was this American visit that led to the change of names that were originally to be given to the new engines. Following the series of Courts, Abbeys, and Castles the next step was to have been a Cathedral class. But when No 6000 was to represent the country, as well as the GWR, in America the name of the reigning sovereign seemed much more appropriate. Incidentally the supply of Cathedrals on the GWR would soon have run out, and names of cathedrals further afield would have had to be used, as was subsequently necessary in a big way with the 'Halls'. I can think of no more than fifteen cathedrals. In addition to various exhibitions there were the famous 5/- (25p) half-day excursions to Swindon. 'The Birthplace of *King George V*'.

Quite apart from all this publicity, which was regarded with a certain amount of mild amusement by those whose railway interests and allegiances lay elsewhere, it soon became apparent that the 'Kings' were extremely powerful and efficient locomotives. That they were restricted as to route was

understandable, and for the first twenty years of their exist-
ence they were confined to the West of England main line via
both Westbury and Bristol, and to between Paddington and
Wolverhampton. They were shedded at Old Oak Common,
Laira and Stafford Road, while a small number were also at
Newton Abbot. For most of the year the Torbay Limited was
a heavy train, incorporating portions to and from Cornwall,
and with the strengthening of the bridges on the branch the
'King' class engines worked through between Paddington and
Kingswear. Full dress dynamometer car trials were conducted
with engine No 6005 *King George II* between Swindon and
Westbury, via Reading West, and the basic coal consump-
tions were even better than those obtained with *Caldicot
Castle* in the epoch-making Swindon–Plymouth trials of 1924.
In terms of coal consumption per train mile the 'Kings' were
heavier than the 'Castles' and the 'Stars' as one would natu-
rally expect them to be. But I remember only too well that a
'whispering campaign' against the 'Kings' went on within the
GWR.

One of my closest personal friends, and a keen student of
locomotive performance, was at that time in the civil engineer's department of the railway, and his duties involved much
travelling between Wolverhampton and Paddington. He told
me of the rumours that were then going the rounds, and how
the 'Kings', because of their heavy coal consumption, were
generally considered to be failures. In view of the much heavier work they were doing it was not surprising that the coal
consumption per train mile was greater, considerably greater
than either 'Castles' or 'Stars'—indeed there would have been
something suspicious about the figures if it had not been so.
But the performance recorded from the footplate by Mr A. V.
Goodyear showed the 'Kings' to be supremely competent engines. Even so, a simple but quite incidental thing strengthened the belief of some that the 'Kings' were not so successful
as the 'Castles'. Up to the end of the year 1930 forty 'Castles'
had been built new, and thirty 'Kings'. After that no more
'Kings' were built, and from 1932 onwards many new 'Castles'
were added. The truth was, of course, that the GWR had as
many 'Kings' as it could economically use, while the policy of
replacement of older 4–6–0 locomotives fitted in well with the

desire to have more 'Castles', with the much higher route availability of that class.

The performances of the original 'Castles' and 'Kings' have been very fully documented in my monograph specially devoted to them, and so far as the 'Castles' were concerned my own finest heavy-load journey was undoubtedly one with the Hawksworth medium-superheat engine No 7036 *Taunton Castle*. That, however, is anticipating the present period by more than twenty years. Some runs with the 'Castles' are discussed in Chapter 10. The 'Kings' in their original low-superheat condition regularly demonstrated their ability to work gross trailing loads of around 530 tons at 70-72mph on level track with regulator wide open, and the usual minimum running cut-offs of 15 to 17 per cent. The superiority over the 'Castles' of the bigger engines can be appreciated by comparing with the details of the dynamometer car test runs conduced with No 4074 *Caldicot Castle* in 1924, the results of which provided the data for Mr Collett's celebrated paper to the World Power Conference in 1925. Engine No 4074 had not been worked to obtain record power outputs; it was rather a demonstration of normal performance. On these tests, hauling a gross trailing load of 480 tons over the level stretches between Bristol and Taunton, the regulator was full open, the cut-off 20 to 22 percent, and the sustained speeds around 65mph. The maximum sustained drawbar horsepower claimed on behalf of *Caldicot Castle* in these conditions was 1000; the 'Kings' output, maintained day after day between Paddington and Reading with the down Cornish Riviera Express was about 1100-1200, on a much earlier cut-off.

The very high nominal tractive effort of the 'Kings' in relation to what seemed a relatively small boiler led some students of locomotive practice to suggest that the 'nominal' tractive effort of 40,300lb was indeed nominal, and that the locomotive could only produce a commensurate power output for brief periods. This was not so. The 'King' boiler, in its original form, with low superheat, was one of the most efficient steam raisers ever put on to a British locomotive in prewar years, and so far as transitory outputs of power were concerned, a few performances on the Birmingham line—made by that incomparable link of the later 1930s, the Stafford Road

Page 81. (above) *West to North express near Worle Junction, engine No 2913 Saint Andrew;* (below) *Bristol–Paddington express, in 1948, leaving Reading, hauled by No 6990* Witherslack Hall

Page 82. (above) *Standard heavy freight 2–8–0 No 2851;* (centre) *the first express freight 2–8–0 No 4700 as fitted with large boiler;* (below) *Laira shed: No 4948* Northwick Hall *and 5ft 8in 2–8–0 No 4703 alongside*

Page 83. (above) *Heavy standard 2–6–2 tank No 3117;* (centre) *a 'County tank' No 2237;* (below) *Standard 2–8–0 tank, No 5217*

Page 84. (above) *Plymouth express approaching Rattery summit: engine No 4070* Neath Abbey; (below) *the 'streamlined' King, No 6014* King Henry VII *approaching Bristol from the west*

No 1—show some astonishing results, when the drawbar pull is compared to the nominal tractive effort of the locomotives.

There is no doubt that a very high degree of skill in firing was practised on the GWR, and to some who were occasionally privileged to ride on the footplate it seemed laborious. The supply of secondary air through the firedoor was always very carefully regulated and it was an almost universal practice to run with the door open, and the steel flap raised. The flap was lowered for each shovelful of coal, and raised again afterwards making a lot of motions to be gone through by the fireman; but it was carried out by a series of slick actions that added little if anything to the labour of firing. In years before World War I a very widely travelled observer of locomotive working from the footplate, who I know was more at home in British Columbia than in Great Britain, made a number of journeys on representative British locomotives and wrote up his experiences afterwards in various journals. He ran with a 'King' on the down Cornish Riviera Express, and was so impressed, unfavourably, with the task of the fireman that he wrote afterwards that the man was working like a Trojan, from start to finish, and concluded—quite wrongly of course —that the coal consumption was very heavy. I have seen 500-ton trains worked on the fastest ordinary timings between Paddington and Newton Abbot on coal consumptions of less than 40lb per train mile. I have often wished that the transatlantic observer who formed such a poor opinion of Great Western locomotives could have been with me on one trip with the up Cornish Riviera Express when the last shovelful of coal was put on when we were still 45 miles from Paddington.

The epic dynamometer car trial runs of 1955 scheduled between Paddington and Plymouth strictly speaking lie outside the period covered by this book. But even when a 'King' class engine was pressed to its utmost and kept at it for nearly three hours on end, the basic coal consumption in pounds per drawbar horsepower hour did not exceed 3.5. In days before World War II when the 'Kings' links at sheds like Old Oak Common, Laira and Stafford Road could be sure of receiving first class coal on each and every day, the Churchward boiler proportions on the 'Kings', with low degree superheat, and the jumper top to the blastpipe, were ideal.

CHAPTER 6

Engine Testing: Dumas and Roberts

THE art of locomotive testing, with dynamometer cars was enormously developed in the last twenty years of steam traction on British Railways, and this development was very largely due to the work done on the Great Western Railway during the grouping period. It was a development of which practically nothing was known at the time outside Swindon, partly because of the cloak of secrecy that surrounded much of the work then in hand, and partly because the Great Western, as previously explained, was somewhat outside the comity of British locomotive affairs. This development covered the vital transition period from the old-style testing traditions of the early Churchward period to the highly scientific, precision methods perfected in British Railways' days by S. O. Ell. The Great Western had been the first of all British railways to own a dynamometer car. Daniel Gooch built one, and used a steam indicator to measure the horsepower of his early broad-gauge locomotives. The results of some of his tests were included in his evidence before the Gauge Commission in 1845. F. W. Webb built a small six-wheeled dynamometer car, which was used on the London & North Western Railway for tests until 1905, but it was Churchward who set the pattern for the more modern and comprehensively equipped cars. Similar ones were built by the North Eastern, the London & North Western, and by the Lancashire and Yorkshire railways.

The trials carried out with the Churchward car prior to World War I were some of the most elaborate yet staged on British metals. Certainly both the North Eastern and the London & North Western carried out many tests, but there was not the same regard for overall efficiency as at Swindon. When the high-power trials with the 'Claughton' class 4–6–0s were conducted in 1913 no measurements were taken of coal consumption! Churchward had been as anxious as anyone to get high power output from his locomotives, but the entire philosophy of Swindon practice was to have locomotives that had a thermal efficiency equal to or better than that of the de Glehn compounds. In the letter to A. V. Goodyear, which I quoted from in Chapter 4, he revealed that his original target of a 2-ton drawbar pull at 70mph had been exceeded with the four-cylinder 4-6-0s, and that $2\frac{1}{2}$ tons at 70mph was their optimum performance. The Great Western was fortunate in one respect for the long level stretches of the original Brunellian main lines induced steady conditions of running which in their turn yielded reliable test results. The Northern companies were more concerned with securing power to climb heavy gradients, and many tests were made on the Shap and Cockburnspath inclines. Churchward wanted power to sustain high speeds with heavy trains on long level stretches of line.

Among engineers of other railways the tasks set to the Great Western were sometimes discounted because of the level nature of many of the principal routes. But while no one would deny that it is essential to have ample tractive effort for working over a hilly route, such a route, which often has alternations of uphill and downhill gradients, can be easier to an ailing engine than one requiring a constant output of power for an hour on end or longer. Furthermore, some of the Great Western routes over which the fastest schedules were operated are particularly exposed to inclement weather. The Bristol main line, for example, has very little shelter if there should be a strong south-westerly wind blowing, while the dead level of the old 'Bristol & Exeter' from Nailsea to Taunton can be a terrible grind, if there is anything of a wind coming off the Severn Sea. Inclement weather apart, however, one was far more likely to get steady boiler and cylinder performance between Southall and Swindon, and between Nailsea and Cogload Junction, and the capacity of a locomotive could be judged with some accuracy. Some tests were carried out on service trains and this was the case with most of the pre-1914 runs, but after the war some of the most important runs originated at Swindon, and were made with specially assembled rakes of empty stock.

The most significant set of trials that had hitherto been conducted on the GWR took place in March 1924, when the new 4–6–0 No 4074 *Caldicot Castle* made three return trips with special trains from Swindon to Plymouth. The trains were made up to the maximum tonnage permitted with a 'Castle' class locomotive over each of the sections concerned, and the best of these three trips gave some coal consumption figures that startled the locomotive world. Made in March, however, there were considerable variations in the weather conditions on the different days, and since the same driver and fireman were concerned, with precisely the same rake of empty coaches, the variations in the actual running were quite extraordinary. The 27 level miles from the foot of the Flax Bourton bank to a point $4\frac{1}{2}$ miles to the south of Bridgwater would, one might imagine, provide a fairly constant test, yet just look at the respective details, as set out in Table 10.

TABLE 10

ENGINE 4074: TESTS IN MARCH 1924

Load: 484 tons tare

Date	14/3/24	19/3/24	25/3/24
	mph	mph	mph
Speed at MP 129	75	71	73
Average MPs 129-138	73.2	68.5	71.3
Average MPs 138-156	64.7	65.7	68.0
Speed at MP 156	62	$65\frac{1}{2}$	68
Cut-offs (with full regulator throughout) %			
at MP 129	25	21	20
at MP 138	22	21	20
at MP 156	22	21	20

On the first run, it will be seen that the use of 25 per cent cut-off persisted to Milepost 138, by which time speed had fallen from 75 to $70\frac{1}{2}$mph. Then a reduction to 22 per cent allowed the speed to fall away to 62mph. Yet on the third run the use of 20 per cent cut-off throughout sustained 68mph almost to the time of shutting off steam for the stop at Taunton. The respective times on the three runs over this 27-mile stretch were: 24min 5sec; 24min 20sec; and 23min 28sec. The fastest time and considerably the highest speed beyond Uphill Junction was made on the trip when the engine was being most lightly worked. A still more remarkable comparison was afforded on two of the return trips, over this same stretch of line, with the same load of 484 tons. The measured length in this case was from Milepost 150 to 133, and on both occasions the engine was working in 20 per cent cut-off, with full regulator, as shown in Table 11.

TABLE 11

Date	March 15	March 20
Average speed for 17 miles (mph)	64.0	55.8
Drawbar Pull (tons)	2.25	2.75
Resistance (total) lb per ton	10.3	12.7
Drawbar horsepower	870	910

This remarkable result indicates that on 20 March, with a strong contrary wind, the train was pulling like 660 tons in calm weather—a 38 per cent increase in the effort required from the locomotive.

These few extracts from a fascinating group of trial results show only too clearly how road conditions can seriously affect locomotive performance in running under what might be termed service requirements. One has to take all that the traffic department and the clerk of the weather puts in one's way. It is sometimes thought that by relating the coal consumption to the actual work done, as registered on the integration apparatus in the dynamometer car, the variables arising from service running conditions are ironed out, and that the basic performance of the locomotive is registered on each and every occasion. But it needed no more than these three return trips from Swindon to Plymouth and back to show that this was not so—with the same engine and crew, working all the time under the most closely observed conditions. Some years ago when engaged on another literary work, I had the privilege of studying the actual dynamometer car records at

Swindon, and then I discovered that the basic coal rate of only 2.83lb per drawbar horsepower hour, that caused such a sensation in British locomotive circles, was achieved on only one of the three round trips. The other two gave rates slightly in excess of 3lb. The best results were obtained on the March 19/20 round. These Great Western results were more consistent than those obtained on the LNER a few years later, when trials were being conducted between Doncaster and Kings Cross, with Gresley 'Pacifics', and one particular engine, worked throughout by the same crew, returned figures of coal per drawbar horsepower hour varying between 2.89 and 3.44 lb—a difference of 19 per cent.

In 1927 a similar set of trials to those of *Caldicot Castle* were carried out with a new 'King' class engine, No 6005 *King George II*, but that time between Swindon and Frome, via Reading. There was no variation in load on this later occasion, and the route gave the chance of some fast steady running, between Shrivenham and Tilehurst, and then the characteristic problems of the Berks and Hants line, with a load equal to the normal maximum of the down Cornish Riviera Express at that time. The best round trip gave a basic coal consumption slightly better than *Caldicot Castle*'s best, but again there was that variation between trips. Although high authority at Swindon was satisfied enough with the results, they set one or two of the more thoughtful younger men wondering. There was something illogical in the fact that the *same* locomotive could yield results of such disparity. These thoughts were no doubt intensified by the results obtained on the LNER in 1928 and published in *The Engineer* not long afterwards. These results naturally attracted much attention at Swindon for they showed that since the Interchange Trials of 1925, which ended in such acrimony between the two companies, the Gresley 'Pacifics' had been so improved that their basic coal consumption was little more than that of the 'Castles' and 'Kings'. If adjustment were made for the slightly lower calorific value of the hard Yorkshire coal supplied to the Doncaster locomotives there would be little significant difference. The best round trips gave 2.89lb per DHP hour for a 180lb 'A1' Pacific, and 2.92lb per DHP hour for a 220lb 'A3'.

The thoughts of younger men at Swindon may not so soon have blossomed into active work had not a request come from the chief engineer for details of the actual speeds necessary to keep certain of the crack express train schedules. The average speeds could of course be worked out from the point-to-point timings laid down, but many of these had remained unchanged for years. They had originally been worked out to discourage exceptionally high speed on the favourable stretches and frequently required, for their strict observance, very rapid starts, and uphill running little slower than specified for some of the downhill stretches. With modern loads such timings had become unrealistic—not in their overall demands, but in their intermediate details. The engineer entrusted with preparation of the speed data required by the chief engineer was C. T. Roberts who later became carriage and wagon engineer of the Western Region of British Railways, and finally chief mechanical and electrical engineer, Scottish Region. From an examination of the results obtained in the trials of *King George II* between Swindon and Frome, in 1927, Roberts was confirmed in his view that locomotives were working at their most efficient when the rate of evaporation in the boiler was constant throughout. Much experience on the footplate had shown also that the best enginemen, from instinct, worked in this way when they had a maximum task of haulage to perform. It was easier for the fireman to maintain a constant head of steam, rather than to try and respond to working by fits and starts as it were. But somewhat naturally the intermediate running times bore little resemblance to those laid down in the working timetable. For example the down Cornish Riviera Express, prior to its acceleration in 1927 had an almost impossible 11min for the initial 9.1 miles out to Southall, and was then required to make average speeds of 62.1mph on to Reading, 56mph up to Savernake and then only 63.7 mph on the racing descent from Savernake to Westbury.

In providing the chief engineer with the data he required Roberts took the boiler and cylinder performance of the *King George II* and, assuming a constant rate of evaporation, worked out a complete set of graphs between Paddington and Exeter in each direction with a load of 500 tons to Westbury, 430 tons to Taunton, and 360 tons beyond, for the down journey. On the up journey the load was taken as 500 tons throughout from Exeter to Paddington. It is interesting to compare in Table 12 the times he worked out on this theoretical basis in relation to those currently in operation with the Cornish Riviera Express.

TABLE 12

CORNISH RIVIERA EXPRESS
Paddington–Exeter

Distance Miles		Actual Sch 1933 min	Estimated times min
0.0	Paddington	0	0
9.1	Southall	11	$12\frac{1}{2}$
18.5	Slough	20	21
36.0	Reading	36	37
53.1	Newbury	54	$55\frac{1}{2}$
66.4	Bedwyn	67	$68\frac{1}{2}$
70.1	Savernake	—	$72\frac{1}{2}$
94.6	Heywood Rd Junction	94	94
102.3	Blatchbridge Junction	—	101
115.1	Castle Cary	$112\frac{1}{2}$	113
140.3	Creech Junction	$135\frac{1}{2}$	135
142.7	Taunton	138	$137\frac{1}{2}$
173.5	Exeter	169	$167\frac{1}{2}$

This shows a more realistic starting time to Southall, and the increase of $1\frac{1}{2}$min is maintained as far as Bedwyn. Then better use of the downhill stretch from Savernake enables the two schedules to draw level at Heywood Road.

The up schedule and estimated times are shown in Table 13. These show the easier running provided for on uphill stretches such as that from Exeter to Taunton, and for harder running downhill, thus approximating more nearly to the principle of running at a constant rate of evaporation.

While the Swindon drawing office was feeling its way towards a new approach to locomotive testing there were nevertheless important stretches of line where the principle of running at an approximate constant rate of evaporation was

Page 93. *Up South Wales–London express climbing from the Severn Tunnel, near Pilning: engine No 5012 Berry Pomeroy Castle*

Page 94. *2.10pm Paddington, Birmingham and North express near Saunderton, engine No 6005* King George II

TABLE 13

CORNISH RIVIERA EXPRESS
Exeter–Paddington

Distance Miles		Actual Sch 1933 min	Estimated times min
0.0	Exeter	0	0
30.8	Taunton	33	$34\frac{1}{2}$
33.2	Creech Junction	—	37
58.4	Castle Cary	61	$61\frac{1}{2}$
71.2	Blatchbridge Junction	—	76
78.9	Heywood Rd Junction	—	$83\frac{1}{2}$
103.4	Savernake	—	$107\frac{1}{2}$
107.1	Bedwyn	112	$111\frac{1}{2}$
120.4	Newbury	124	124
137.5	Reading	142	$141\frac{1}{2}$
155.0	Slough	159	159
164.4	Southall	168	$167\frac{1}{2}$
173.5	Paddington	179	179

impracticable, and where the impact of purely theoretical considerations had some odd results. Passing forward, so far as this subject is concerned, to the year 1935, the inception of the high-speed Bristolian express, to mark the centenary of the company, was followed by strong representations for a similar service to Birmingham. Although the route was not so continuously favourable the distance was 8 miles less, and the request for a non-stop express in $1\frac{3}{4}$ hours seemed reasonable in every way. In the few years between the opening of this route, in 1910, and the onset of World War I there had been little opportunity to work up a traffic, in opposition to the well-established standards of the London & North Western, or to work up any firm traditions. Loads were for the most part fairly light, and locomotives varied from 4–4–0s and de Glehn compounds to both classes of 4–6–0. But when the 2-hour trains were reinstated, in the autumn of 1921, the 'Star' class engines were employed practically to the exclusion of all others. Loads were much heavier, and a very high standard of performance was quickly established. Speeds of 80 to 85mph on the down grades became, as one commentator

95

expressed it, 'as plentiful as the blackberries in the autumn'; there were occasional 'nineties', and those of us who were compiling logs found it all most exhilarating. What some of us did not realise, however, was the frequency with which official speed limits were being exceeded, and no less the frequency with which locomotives, by official reckonings, were being overloaded.

The Great Western had its own ways of making rules, and some ingenious ways of breaking them! For example, on the 2-hour Birmingham expresses making one intermediate stop the load limit for a 'Star' was 320 tons. Yet anyone taking an early evening stroll round Paddington in the mid-1920s would see the 6.10pm express pulling out, night after night, with a tare load of over 400 tons. And no one in their wildest dreams ever thought of asking for a pilot. I was given to understand that with a 320-ton load a driver was expected to adhere strictly to the point-to-point times laid down in the working timetable; with heavier trains it was hoped that he would reach Leamington on time, but no one enquired into the game of 'swings and roundabouts' by which he 'bent' the intermediate timings in order to do this. I have before me details of two runs on which *Princess Alice* and *Queen Adelaide* left Paddington with loads of 425 and 440 tons respectively, and made net times of 89½ and 89min to Leamington, against a schedule of 91min for this run of 87.3 miles. On the 3.54pm up from Banbury (the 3.0pm out of Birmingham) *Bath Abbey* and *King James* kept the 70min timing to Paddington (67.5 miles) with loads of 445 and 460 tons respectively. It was only when the load on this same train reached 453 tons *tare*, about 490 tons full, that the driver of a 'Star' class engine failed to keep time. How was it done? There were times when certain of the speed limits were interpreted rather freely; but going through Aynho Junction at 70mph instead of 55, and taking High Wycombe at 45 instead of 35mph was not going to make up the tremendous discrepancy between the official load limit, and what drivers regularly undertook without the slightest question.

The explanation was, of course, that the Birmingham route was an ideal one for practising the art of mortgaging the boiler. On the down journey, for example, a driver and fireman could throw in all they had to make a very fast ascent of the Gerrards Cross bank, and if they had lost pressure and water level in so doing, the descent from Beaconsfield to High Wycombe and the brief interlude of running without steam preparatory to the slack there enabled the boiler conditions to be restored, if, as usual, the engine was steaming freely. Then one could take another tremendous 'bash' at Saunderton bank. The engine could be worked briefly at a steam rate that could not be sustained indefinitely, and the ascent would be brilliant; but this was a method of working that cannot be reduced to precise figures. The drawing office would disregard any such capabilities, as being merely transitory. It is true enough that such work was a matter of footplate psychology as much as anything else. Not every driver and fireman would be prepared to make the effort; but such running became almost a point of honour with the Wolverhampton No 1 link, and those of us who travelled at all regularly on the Birmingham trains took such performance for granted. I have described this situation at some length in order to explain the rather defeatist attitude that seemed to be assumed at Swindon when the suggestion for a $1\frac{3}{4}$-hour Birmingham service was put up.

I should add that the Wolverhampton No 1 link continued the good work with the 'Kings'. In the famous 1953 trials with engine No 6001 *King Edward VII* when that engine was steamed continuously at 30,000lb per hour, and required two firemen to do it, the drawbar horsepower at 55mph was 1,440; yet on six runs of the 1930-39 period, on ordinary service trips with the 6.10pm out of Paddington, the calculated drawbar horsepower at the summit of the Saunderton bank were 1,642, 1,815, 1,785, 1,761, 1,694 and 1,676. When Swindon analysed the possibilities of the $1\frac{3}{4}$-hour Birmingham service they could only take the proven capacity of the 'Kings' in continuous steaming, and the graphs they prepared, based again on the 1927 trials with *King George 11*, showed that it was just possible to make a $1\frac{3}{4}$-hour run, non-stop, with a 300-ton train, and that with 400 tons there was little margin on a 2-hour schedule with one intermediate stop! Nothing remotely matching the maximum efforts just quoted was envisaged, while it had also been laid down, apparently, that the maximum speeds were not to exceed 80mph at any point. On the run when the output of 1,785 was made on the Saunderton bank, as quoted earlier, the descent to Haddenham was taken at 91½mph! But in every way the Paddington–Birmingham service of the inter-war years was a phenomenon never equalled anywhere before or since.

While the work of C. T. Roberts was leading Swindon towards the principle of testing locomotives at constant rates of evaporation, rather than constant speed, another very important development in testing was taking place. Sir Nigel Gresley, as chief mechanical engineer of the LNER was a constant advocate of the need for a modern well-equipped stationary testing plant in Great Britain. In the chronically depressed state of LNER finances it was unlikely that the capital necessary to provide such an installation would be forthcoming from the one company; yet he succeeded, very publicly, in emphasising the lack of any such plant by getting authority to send his big 2–8–2 *Cock o' the North* to the French plant at Vitry-sur-Seine. When Stanier went to the LMS, Gresley sought and obtained his backing for a national plant, with costs to be shared, and then the two engineers thought that the cost might be further reduced if the Great Western came into it as well. From his long experience at Swindon Stanier knew of the limited capacity of the old 'home trainer', and assumed it would not be of any account for modern purposes. But at Swindon itself in the development of the idea of testing at constant rates of evaporation it was appreciated that the stationary plant could play an important part. Accordingly in 1935 a scheme of modernisation had been authorised that dispensed with the old air-compressor plant for absorbing power, and from being restricted to the development of about 500 horsepower the plant, by the introduction of new equipment, could absorb the maximum output of any existing Great Western locomotive. There is a good story than when Stanier and Sir Nigel Gresley jointly approached the Great Western to participate in the project of a new plant, their representatives were invited to Swindon and shown the 4–6–0 *Arlington Court* going flat-out on the modernised plant. That was the end of any ideas of getting the GWR to participate! The plant, as reconstructed, became of immense importance to the nationalised British Railways.

CHAPTER 7

Swan Song of the 6ft 8½in 4-4-0s

A T the time of grouping the Great Western still had its complete stud of 6ft 8½in express passenger 4–4–0s, save for one. There had been originally six different classes, though by 1922 these had been rationalised into three. The six original classes and their respective strengths were:

'Armstrong'	4
'Badminton'	20
'Atbara'	40
'City'	10
'County'	40
'Flower'	20

The four 'Armstrongs', with small domed boilers that made them like a 4–4–0 version of the famous Dean 7ft 8in singles, originally had 7ft diameter coupled wheels. The 'Badmintons', were built new with much larger domed boilers and Belpaire fireboxes. But by 1922 the 'Armstrongs', 'Badmintons' and 'Atbaras' had been assimilated to the 'Flower' class, using the Swindon standard No 2 tapered domeless boiler, while the 'Cities' and the 'Counties' had the larger No 4 standard. The 'Atbaras' as previously mentioned had their numbers reduced by one in 1911, when the engine *Mafeking* was involved in the accident at Henley-in-Arden, and was so badly damaged as to be not worth repairing. Ten other 'Atbaras' were rebuilt with No 4 boilers and were transferred to the 'City' class. Thus at the time of grouping the 4–4–0 stud, having 6ft 8½in coupled wheels was as follows:

'Flower'	73
'City'	20
'County'	40

The names and numbers of the first two classes are included in tables at the end of this chapter. It was not a large stud for so big a railway as the Great Western, though of course a great deal of the work on the hilly, more remote sections of the system was being done by 5ft 8½in 4–4–0s of the 'Bulldog' and 'Duke' classes, of which there were 140 and 39 respectively.

The grouping era had not progressed very far, however, before it was evident that the days of the inside cylinder 6ft 8½in 4–4–0s were numbered. In 1927 to the horror of Great Western enthusiasts six engines of the 'Badminton' series, ten 'Atbaras', six of the purely 'Flower' series of 1908, and one 'City' were scrapped. I remember the reaction to it all the more vividly from an incident that took place in the old shop of the Locomotive Publishing Company at Amen Corner. In Walter Bell's time that shop sometimes partook of the character of a club house, where railway enthusiasts met to gossip, as well as to buy postcards and such like. I called in one day and found a certain *habitué* almost in tears at the news of some Great Western scrappings. It was microscopic compared to the slaughters we have witnessed in recent years; but I remember him exclaiming: 'At the rate things are going there will not be a four-coupled engine left in the country in a few years!' And that was in 1927. In the meantime those that were left were continuing to do much good work. At that time the Bristol–Birmingham route was worked entirely by 4–4–0 locomotives, and while the outside-cylindered 'Counties' had a monopoly of the more important turns, 'Cities' and 'Flowers' were called upon as relief and reserve engines. Nevertheless by the end of 1929 only three 'Cities', seven 'Badmintons', six 'Atbaras', four 'Flowers', and one 'Armstrong' remained. It was at this stage that the movement to save the *City of Truro* from the scrapheap got under way.

The 'County' class was then still intact. Those sturdy outside-cylindered engines have been described as the least successful of all the Churchward standard classes. With this I would certainly not agree. They were designed for a specified purpose, and they fulfilled that purpose admirably. At the turn of the century the important and rapidly developing service over the West to North route via the Severn Tunnel was being worked mainly by the 'Badminton' class 4–4–0s, assisted by the inside-framed '3232' class of 2–4–0s. Maintenance for the joint line between Hereford and Shrewsbury was then the responsibility of the LNWR, and there were certain weight restrictions. Unlike the situation that prevailed in later days, when the entire express service was worked by the GWR, some trains were then worked by the North Western, and the largest engines were then Webb 4-cylinder compound 4–4–0s of the modified 'Alfred the Great' class, then usually known as the 'Benbows'. The story goes that Churchward would like to have tried out some of his new 4–6–0s over that heavy road, but that such a proposal, if it was actually made, was vetoed on account of weight by the LNWR civil engineer. So instead he produced a 4–4–0 version of the new 4–6–0, with identical cylinders and motion, and using the 'City' or Swindon No 4 standard boiler. The 'Counties', with Churchward's own setting of the Stephenson link motion, had the same exceptional ability to climb heavy gradients at low or medium speed, though they needed careful handling in order not to run them short of steam.

Again, however, as with the maximum uphill efforts of the four-cylinder 4–6–0s on the Birmingham line much could be done by exploiting the technique of mortgaging the boiler. There was, however, a rather significant difference between the North to West route and the Birmingham line, in that the profile of the former included considerably longer gradients, with less of a switchback characteristic. It was, for example, a case of almost continuous collar work between Hereford and Church Stretton, going north, and a long pull of nearly twelve miles from Shrewsbury up to Church Stretton going south. Much the same characteristics were to be found in the gradients of the Birmingham–Bristol route, particularly in the lengthy adverse stretch from Bearley up to Earlswood Lakes in the northbound direction. Nevertheless the enginemen became very expert in handling the 'Counties' in these conditions, as details of a few typical runs will later show. Although considerably more powerful the 'Counties' were not such steady or comfortable engines as the 'Cities', and it was probably their rough riding more than anything else that induced a lower standard of maximum speed. I have not seen a maximum speed recorded of more than 82mph with a 'County', whereas the 'Cities' in their prime—and the 'Atbaras' too— used to dash up to 90mph with very little inducement, quite apart from spurts like those of the Ocean Mail trains. But the great merit of the 'Counties' lay in their great power at low speeds, arising from the setting of the Stephenson link motion, as explained in Chapter 4.

Reverting now to the inside cylinder engines a few personal recollections of the 1920s may be interspersed. In my travels on the GWR, and in photographic expeditions to various parts of the line I saw many of these engines, and can only regret that in 1926 I did not keep records of those that were regularly working between Bristol and Salisbury. The last survivor of the 'Armstrongs', No 4169 *Brunel*, was then stationed at Bristol, Bath Road shed, and certainly putting in a good deal of mileage on secondary services. I saw her frequently at Temple Meads and once, in 1925, she gave me the surprise of my life, by coming bowling out of Marley Tunnel on the South Devon line, dashing past Rattery signal box at a full 60mph with an all-stations local from Plymouth to Newton Abbot. She was not heavily loaded, but her acceleration from Brent must have been fierce for her to pass Rattery, only 2¾ miles distant, at the speed she did. At the same time No 3715 *City of Hereford* was working from Reading, often on the faster commuter trains to and from Paddington. But as far as I was concerned the happiest hunting ground for these much loved engines was north of Birmingham. I used to see No 3708 *Killarney*, taking the Birkenhead portions of London expresses north of Shrewsbury and it was in this area too that the immortal *City of Truro* finished her ordinary working life.

Looking back it is not difficult now to appreciate the distress of enthusiasts of an older generation at witnessing the scrapping of these old favourites. At that time, for men of my own age, there was so much new to be followed up all over the country, and there were my own personal interests in the technical aspects of locomotive performance, that I am only too well aware, now, of having treated the scrapping of old engines as just one of those things. A determined assault had not then commenced against the 'Bulldogs', but somehow or

other, even in those days, the 'Bulldogs' did not seem to in-
spire the same affection as the 6ft 8½in engines. All this may
sound rather sentimental, and apart from the plain facts of
GWR Steam in the grouping era. But I do not think the locomotives of any railway have inspired greater affection from so
many people than those of the Great Western, and it is perhaps just permissible to drop the metaphorical tear when
writing once again of the last days of the 'Badmintons', 'Atbaras', 'Flowers' and 'Cities'—not forgetting the four 'Armstrongs'. In those last days the majority of them were running
in plain unlined green, and their safety-valve covers were
painted over and had cast iron chimneys. Only a few, so far
as my observations go, had their old copper tops burnished,
and their safety valves bright. *City of Hereford* was an exception and always looked a picture whenever I saw her.

As to their actual work in the closing years, 'Flower' class
engines were usually employed on the afternoon express from
South Wales to Birmingham. Although the load was normally
no more than those of the Ocean Mails of old this train for
some reason had an easier schedule than that of the 'crack'
Penzance–Wolverhampton express, being allowed 37min for
the 29.1 miles from Cheltenham to Stratford-on-Avon and
32min for the concluding 25 miles into Birmingham. From
Cheltenham up to Winchcombe there is a continuous ascent
at 1 in 150-200, and then the gradients are favourable mostly
into Stratford. The only intermediate hindrance was the permanent speed restriction of 40mph over the Honeybourne
Junctions. Details are set out in Table 14 of two runs on this
train, when slightly late starts from Cheltenham encouraged
the drivers to make unusually fast times to Stratford. On the
first of these two runs No 4142 *Brisbane*, originally an 'Atbara', went magnificently up to Winchcombe sustaining 56-
57mph on the 1 in 150, and then reached 80mph on the
descent to Honeybourne. As was so often the case in that era,
the Honeybourne restriction was observed more in the spirit
than by the letter. *Brisbane* skated over the junction at little
below 60mph and then went easily on to Stratford, not ex-
ceeding 66mph. Even so, to reach Stratford in no more than
29min 16sec from Cheltenham was an exciting piece of work.
On the companion run, engine No 4140, one of the very few

TABLE 14

'Atbara' Class Engines

Locomotive No			4142	4140
Locomotive Name			*Brisbane*	(Adelaide)
Load tons E/F			106/110	112/115
Distance		Sch	Actual	Actual
Miles		min	min sec	min sec
0.0	CHELTENHAM	0	0 00	0 00
4.1	Bishops Cleeve		5 46	5 53
9.0	Winchcombe		10 48	10 50
11.6	Toddington		13 11	13 21
16.1	Broadway		17 02	17 43
18.8	Weston-sub-Edge		19 09	20 08
21.1	*Honeybourne East*			
	Junction	26	21 00	22 14
29.1	STRATFORD-ON-AVON	37	29 16	30 23
2.6	Wilmcote		4 31	5 07
4.3	*Bearley North*			
	Junction		6 18	—
8.0	HENLEY-IN-ARDEN	13	10 12	10 38
14.8	Earlswood Lakes		19 01	18 18
17.7	Shirley	22	22 42	21 08
20.2	Hall Green		25 19	23 40
21.7	Tyseley	27	27 22	26 05
—			slack	sigs.
25.0	BIRMINGHAM	32	32 20	33 58

unnamed engines, was little slower up to Winchcombe sustaining 56mph, but she did not exceed 69mph down to Honeybourne. Once again, however, the junction was taken at a full 60mph.

There is a very awkward start out of Stratford-on-Avon, with 1¼ miles at 1 in 75 up to Wilmcote. This is followed by three miles of slightly falling gradient to the foot of Henley bank—9 miles long, all at 1 in 150, until the last 2 miles, when the inclination eases to 1 in 181. *Brisbane*, having got back to schedule by her fast running from Cheltenham, took things moderately and after touching 65mph past Bearley fell to 42mph at Wood End Halt. A maximum of 68mph was attained before the very severe slack at Tyseley. The unnamed engine No 4140 did splendidly. She also attained 65mph at Bearley, but did not fall below 51mph on the 1 in 150 gradient. Although the loads were light for the period these were two sparkling runs, and show what the 'Atbaras' could still do, even though their scrapping was to come so soon afterwards. As a matter of interest I may add that No 4140 when originally built in 1901 was No 3394, one of the 3393–3412 series of 'Atbaras' named after cities of the British Empire. No 3394 was *Adelaide*, but the name was removed in 1910 to avoid confusion with the new 4-cylinder 4–6–0 No 4034 *Queen Adelaide*.

I have set out in Table 15 details of another fast run with an engine of this same series No 4147 *St Johns* in the reverse

TABLE 15

GWR BIRMINGHAM–CHELTENHAM
Load: 171 tons tare, 180 tons full
Engine: 4–4–0 No 4147 *St Johns*

Distance Miles		Sch min	Actual min sec
0.0	BIRMINGHAM	0	0 00
3.3	Tyseley	5	5 56
5.8	Hall Green		8 35
7.3	Shirley		11 50
10.2	Earlswood Lakes		15 16
17.0	HENLEY-IN-ARDEN	20	21 48
20.7	*Bearley North Junction*	24	25 14
22.4	Wilmcote		27 00
25.0	STRATFORD-ON-AVON	31	30 30
3.0	Milcote		4 44
8.0	*Honeybourne East Junction*	10	10 07
10.3	Weston-sub-Edge		12 31
13.0	Broadway		15 19
17.5	Toddington		19 52
20.1	Winchcombe		22 26
25.0	Bishops Cleeve		27 30
29.1	CHELTENHAM	33	32 31

direction over this route. A rather heavier load was conveyed. Speed was reduced to 30mph over the junctions at Tyseley, and the rising length to Earlswood Lakes was taken at 50-51 mph, on gradients mostly around 1 in 200. Down Henley bank speeds ranged up to 70mph, but with numerous slight reductions. There was some very good running up the long rise to Winchcombe, with a sustained 54mph up the 1 in 200 to Broadway, and the smart timing of 32min then allocated to this train was nicely maintained. It was not usual to put the inside cylinder engines on to the West of England expresses but, as I have shown, on the Birmingham–South Wales trains, and equally on the holiday expresses between Birmingham and Weston-super-Mare, these engines continued to do excellent work. It was the same on the north road from Shrewsbury. Engine No 3715 *City of Chester*, working a 265-ton load on one of the fastest of the Birkenhead–Paddington expresses, made a very smart run from Ruabon. Getting away well and touching 64mph on the Dee viaduct below Cefn, she went up the 2½ miles of 1 in 142 to Preesgweene at the notable minimum speed of 51mph and passed Gobowen, 7.6 miles, in 9min 40sec from the dead start. On the sharply undulating length to Baschurch a general average of around 60mph was maintained, with an easy maximum of 66mph near Rednal, and despite signal checks at the finish there was time in hand for a punctual arrival in Shrewsbury, 25.6 miles in 30¾min from Ruabon, or 28½min net. In the reverse direction No 3711 *City of Birmingham* worked a train of 175 tons to Ruabon in 29½min start to stop, against the general rising tendency of the line.

City of Birmingham was withdrawn in 1930, leaving only the *City of Bristol* and the *City of Truro* of this famous class. Eleven more of the 'Flowers' were scrapped, these including four original 'Badmintons', three 'Atbaras', three original 'Flowers' and the celebrated 4169 *Brunel*. In the following year the last of them were withdrawn. As a matter of sentimental interest I add the names and numbers of the last survivors of this group of locomotives:

4109   *Monarch*
4113   *Samson*

4115 *Shrewsbury*
4132 *Pembroke*
4145 *Dunedin*
4148 *Singapore*
4150 *Begonia*
3712 *City of Bristol*

The first three were originally 'Badmintons', and the next three were originally 'Atbaras'. In the meantime, of course, No 3717 *City of Truro* had been presented to the York Railway Museum, in March 1931. Although this melancholy subject of scrapping is dealt with in more detail under the individual classes, I may add that the year 1931 saw not only the withdrawal of twenty-nine 'County' class 4–4–0s which, added to the six withdrawn in 1930, left only five of them in traffic at the end of 1931, but more surprising was the scrapping of three 'Saint' class 4–6–0s—*Lady of Provence, Lady of Shalott*, and *Peveril of the Peak.*

Little did I imagine, however, when I saw 'Cities' and 'Atbaras' going about their last ordinary duties in the late 1920s, and learning of their withdrawal not long afterwards, that some twenty-five years later I should have the opportunity of riding on the footplate of a 'City' class 4–4–0 on a first class express schedule. But as all Great Western enthusiasts know the *City of Truro* was exhumed from the precincts of York in 1957, and after a most thorough-going overhaul at Swindon ran a considerable mileage on special trains in that summer, and also in Scotland during the following year. In her last year in ordinary traffic the engine had a No 4 standard boiler, superheated with top feed, and when she went to York in 1931 she was finished in the standard livery for express passenger locomotives at that time, fully lined out, with Great Western in full and the gartered crest on her tender. But when she was overhauled at Swindon, in 1957, someone had the inspiration of restoring the highly decorative original livery of 1903, with Indian red underframes and a more elaborate system of lining out. This also involved the three-panel style of painting on the tender, with the elaborate weaving of the letters GWR into a scroll device on the centre panel. Beautiful as that colour scheme looked in 1957 it did not

107

entirely meet the approval of certain elderly and most erudite enthusiasts, who knew Great Western locomotives when the entire stud was painted thus. There were, inevitably perhaps, certain details of the lining out in which the restorers had erred, but these were *minutiae*, and the general effect was glorious.

I must admit, however, that when I was favoured with a footplate pass to ride the *City of Truro* on a Sunday excursion from Bath to Kingswear and back I expected that it would be little more than a nostalgic occasion, and nothing remotely resembling hard express running would be attempted; but the excursions worked by this engine were proving so popular that a train of eight modern coaches was provided. Practically every seat was taken, and we had a load of fully 285 tons behind the tender. In this connection it is important to remember that when the 'Cities' were in their prime the loads of the crack express trains they worked were mostly less than 200 tons. The Ocean Mail special on which *City of Truro* made her record run, was loaded to 148 tons. The excursion train originated at Swindon, and when I boarded the engine at Bath all was going well. In the short run from Bath to Bristol she rode beautifully, and steamed well; moreover, it was quite evident that those on her footplate cherished no thoughts about the tender handling of a museum piece. She was a working engine and she was going to have to *work*. There were a number of checks on the outward journey, because of relaying, and on account of the water troughs at Creech Junction being under repair; but the way that 'museum piece' got away from the water stop at Taunton and climbed to Whiteball tunnel was most impressive, and it was then that my friends on the footplate disclosed what they had in mind for the return journey. The train was booked to run non-stop from Teignmouth to Bristol, and they were intending to go for a really high maximum speed down the Wellington bank.

Between Newton Abbot and Kingswear the engine somewhat naturally needed assistance over the heavy gradients of the branch. One of the big '51XX' 2-6-2 tanks were coupled on for this purpose and by arrangement we left her to do most of the work. But on returning to Newton Abbot in the evening, and the Bristol driver and fireman taking over again, all was ready for the big attempt. Inspector Andress had travelled with the engine throughout from Swindon, and he pronounced her in first-rate nick. The log of our splendid run is shown in Table 16. We got vigorously away from Teignmouth, but then with the need for easing round the Starcross

TABLE 16

WESTERN REGION: TEIGNMOUTH–BRISTOL

An Excursion in 1957

Load: 8 coaches, 264 tons tare, 285 tons full
Engine: 4–4–0 No 3440 *City of Truro*

Distance Miles		Actual min sec	Speeds mph
0.0	TEIGNMOUTH	0 00	—
2.8	Dawlish	5 05	50
6.5	Starcross	9 18	(slack)
10.3	Exminster	13 22	62
15.0	EXETER	18 42	35*
18.5	Stoke Canon	23 17	52
22.2	Silverton	27 29	56/53
27.6	Cullompton	33 18	56
29.9	Tiverton Junction	36 00	47½/54½
32.9	*Milepost 176*	39 34	50
34.9	*Whiteball Box*	42 23	38
38.7	Wellington	46 08	84
43.8	Norton Fitzwarren	50 05	72
—		slack	
45.8	TAUNTON	52 52	25*
51.6	Durston	59 23	60/57
57.3	BRIDGWATER	65 08	62/56
63.6	Highbridge	71 23	61
66.4	Brent Knoll	74 08	59
73.8	*Worle Junction*	81 30	61½
78.6	YATTON	86 15	62
84.6	Flax Bourton	92 27	50
88.7	Parson St	96 55	58(max)
90.6	BRISTOL (TEMPLE MEADS)	101 25	

* Speed restrictions

109

curves and to top up the tender 'to the brim' at Exminster troughs nothing unusual happened until we were through Exeter. Then came a fine climb to Whiteball, with the engine working with regulator full open and 27 per cent cut-off until we were past Tiverton Junction. Although the engine was opened out to 33 per cent at this stage, for the final part of the ascent to Whiteball there was still plenty in reserve; she could have been pushed harder if necessary, but my friends on the footplate wanted plenty of steam for what was to follow. Even so, full regulator and 33 per cent was hard work for a museum piece, and speed dropped only from 50mph to 38mph in the two miles of 1 in 115 gradient leading to Whiteball Tunnel.

On her great run of 9 May 1904, *City of Truro* topped Whiteball Summit at 52mph with a load of 148 tons; we were doing 38mph with a load of 285 tons, and although we did not reach the 'ton' we certainly touched 84mph and averaged 82.8mph from Wellington station to Bradford Crossing. Approaching Taunton, however, we had to slow down to cross from main to relief line. Because of the quadrupling and the present layout at Cogload it is now only the direct London trains that get a high-speed run through Taunton. The Bristol line leads off the relief line at Cogload, and had we not crossed over at Taunton we should have had to do so at Cogload. On the basis of running practice in the days when the *City of Truro* was new this crossover slack cost us about 2½min in running. The open, exposed stretches of line along the Somersetshire coastal plain lived up to their reputation and provided us with a strong cross-wind. It needed hard work, with full regulator and 26 per cent cut-off to yield an average speed of 58.8mph over the 37.9 miles from Durston to Bedminster; but we finished into Bristol in 101min 25sec from Teignmouth, with an average speed of 54mph, with a load of 285 tons. Some 'museum piece'!

And so I come finally to the 'Counties'. Once the civil engineering authorities of the LMSR were prepared to accept the 'Saint' class 4-6-0s over the old West of England main line of the Midland, between Standish Junction and Yate there was no longer any need for these engines. The 'slaughter' commenced in 1930 and, as previously mentioned, there were only seven out of the original forty engines of this class left on

Page 111. (above) *Cornish Riviera Express near Reading West, in 1947, engine No 6025* King Henry III, *with the author on the footplate;* (below) *1.30pm Paddington–Penzance express near Southcote Junction: 'streamlined' 4–6–0 No 6014* King Henry VII

Page 112. (above) *Paddington–Ilfracombe express climbing Mortehoe bank: a 'Bulldog' 4–4–0, assisted in rear by an ex-*LSWR *'M7' 0–4–4 tank;* (below) *Newcastle–Bournemouth express near Tilehurst (ex-*GCR *stock): engine No 4102* Blenheim, *'Badminton' class*

New Year's Day 1932. The last survivors were:

3803	*County Cork*
3812	*County of Cardigan*
3814	*County of Chester*
3815	*County of Hants*
3822	*County of Brecon*
3829	*County of Merioneth*
3834	*County of Somerset*

The 'County' class engines were regularly used on the 5.30am semi-fast train from Paddington to Bristol in the late 1920s, and I logged No 3803 *County Cork* on this job, with a 320-ton train in the late summer of 1926. Engines 3808 *County Limerick* and 3810 *County Wicklow* were at Bristol at this same time. The former engine caught me napping one Saturday afternoon at Corsham in 1926. With a push--bicycle for transport I was exploring the district and intending to clock-in at the line side in time to photograph the up Ilfracombe Express, which then ran via Bristol and made a non-stop run from Bath to Paddington. But I got a puncture and my progress was somewhat delayed, and I arrived at the overbridge just to the west of Corsham station as the train emerged from Box Tunnel. There was no time to select a suitable spot, and in the excitement of seeing what was approaching I did get a 'record', but that was the most charitable view one could take of the resulting photograph. That train was *double-headed*, with *County Limerick* piloting a 'Saint', the *Bride of Lammermoor*. Only once before had I ever seen an important express double-headed east of Newton Abbot, and that was on another Saturday when *Morning Star* had taken the third portion of the down Cornish Riviera Express, and came back as a pilot to the 4.12pm from Taunton. Whether *County Limerick* went through to Paddington on that other occasion I don't know, but they had an enormous train between them.

So far as the Birmingham–Bristol line is concerned, details are tabulated of a good run by the *County of Hereford*, on the 'Penzance' (see Table 17). It was generally understood that considerably heavier loads than this were sometimes taken without assistance; but I have not seen a definite record in print of any such occasion. The engine was starting 'cold' out

G

TABLE 17
GWR BRISTOL–BIRMINGHAM
Load: 275 tons tare, 295 tons full
Engine: 4–4–0 No 3828 *County of Hereford*

Distance Miles		Sch min	Actual min sec	Speeds mph
0.0	STAPLETON ROAD	0	0 00	—
3.2	Filton Junction		9 26	20 (min)
8.9	*Westerleigh West Junction*	15	17 49	47/20*
—			sigs.	
10.3	Yate	19	22 36	—
15.1	Wickwar		29 08	—
22.2	Berkeley Road		35 07	73
24.6	Coaley		37 20	61
28.5	Stonehouse		40 56	64
30.1	*Standish Junction*	39	42 46	44*
37.3	*Engine Shed Junction*	51	50 32	64/45*
39.7	Churchdown		53 40	49
43.1	CHELTENHAM	60	58 49	
4.1	Bishops Cleeve		7 52	41½
9.0	Winchcombe		14 15	—
11.6	Toddington		16 49	—
16.1	Broadway		21 02	70
21.1	*Honeybourne East Junction*	24	25 34	59*
26.1	Milcote		30 08	72
29.1	STRATFORD-ON-AVON	34	33 37	
2.6	Wilmcote		5 23	
4.3	*Bearley North Junction*	7	—	64
8.0	HENLEY-IN-ARDEN	11	11 11	46 (min)
14.8	Earlswood Lakes		19 28	48
17.7	Shirley	21	22 34	—
20.2	Hall Green		24 54	68
21.7	Tyseley	26	26 50	
—			slack	
25.0	BIRMINGHAM	31	32 10	

* Speed restrictions

of Bristol, and fell to 20mph on Filton Bank (1 in 75), and with a bad signal check at the entry to the Midland line the train was 5min late at Berkeley Road; but some smart running followed and Cheltenham was reached 1min early. On restarting, the ascent to Winchcombe was naturally somewhat slower than those of the 'Atbaras' referred to earlier in this chapter. But the *County of Hereford* made some good speed afterwards and Stratford was reached on time. Extremely good work was done on the final stage with a minimum speed of 46mph up the long 1 in 150 past Henley-in-Arden, and a fast concluding run down from Earlswood to Tyseley. The working over this route was indeed the swan-song of the 'Counties' and the moment the LMS were prepared to accept the 'Saints' over their part of the line the whole 'County' class was called in, as fast as the scrapyard at Swindon could take them. Actually it was not the 'Saints' that superseded the 'Counties' on this important north to west route, but the new 6ft 4-6-0s of the 'Hall' class. By August 1931 no fewer than 121 of these most useful engines were in service.

'Flower' class: I 'Badminton' series—

4100	*Badminton*	4110	*Charles Mortimer*
4101	*Barrington*	4111	*Marlborough*
4102	*Blenheim*	4112	*Oxford*
4103	*Bessborough*	4113	*Samson*
4104	*Cambria*	4114	*Shelburne*
4105	*Earl Cawdor*	4115	*Shrewsbury*
4106	*Grosvenor*	4116	*Savernake*
4107	*Alexander Hubbard*	4117	*Shakespeare*
4108	*Hotspur*	4118	*Waterford*
4109	*Monarch*	4119	*Wynnstay*

'Flower' class: II 'Atbara' series—

4120	*Atbara*	4126	*Kimberley*
4121	*Baden Powell*	4127	*Ladysmith*
4122	*Colonel Edgcumbe*	4128	*Maine*
4123	—	4129	*Kekewich*
4124	*Kitchener*	4130	*Omdurman*
4125	*Khartoum*	4131	*Powerful*

4132	*Pembroke*	4141	*Aden*
4133	*Roberts*	4142	*Brisbane*
4134	*Sir Redvers*	4143	*Cape Town*
4135	*Pretoria*	4144	*Colombo*
4136	*Terrible*	4145	*Dunedin*
4137	*Wolseley*	4146	*Sydney*
4138	*White*	4147	*St Johns*
4139	*Auckland*	4148	*Singapore*
4140	—		

'Flower' class: III Flowers proper—

4149	*Auricula*	4159	*Anemone*
4150	*Begonia*	4160	*Carnation*
4151	*Calceolaria*	4161	*Hyacinth*
4152	*Calendula*	4162	*Marguerite*
4153	*Camellia*	4163	*Marigold*
4154	*Campanula*	4164	*Mignonette*
4155	*Cineraria*	4165	*Narcissus*
4156	*Gardenia*	4166	*Polyanthus*
4157	*Lobelia*	4167	*Primrose*
4158	*Petunia*	4168	*Stephanotis*

Flower class: IV 'Armstrongs'—

4169	*Brunel*	4171	*Armstrong*
4170	*Charles Saunders*	4172	*Gooch*

'City' class: 4-4-0s—

3700	*Durban*	3710	*City of Bath*
3701	*Gibraltar*	3711	*City of Birmingham*
3702	*Halifax*	3712	*City of Bristol*
3703	*Hobart*	3713	*City of Chester*
3704	*Lyttleton*	3714	*City of Gloucester*
3705	*Mauritius*	3715	*City of Hereford*
3706	*Melbourne*	3716	*City of London*
3707	*Malta*	3717	*City of Truro*
3708	*Killarney*	3718	*City of Winchester*
3709	*Quebec*	3719	*City of Exeter*

CHAPTER 8

Derivatives from Churchward Standards

APART from comparatively brief references to the 'Castles' and 'Kings', the design and construction of which has been so fully documented elsewhere, I have so far concerned myself in this book with the continuing good work of locomotives that were already in existence at the time of grouping, and it is now necessary to turn to the new engines of other than first line express passenger types. These can be classified broadly into two groups, those that are derived from Churchward standards, in that they all have the domeless taper boiler, and the majority also the basic two-cylinder engine layout; the second group all have domed boilers, inside cylinders and are not superheated. The first group can conveniently include the standard South Wales tank engine, introduced in 1924 to provide a standard unit for use on all the amalgamated and absorbed railways. The other inside-cylindered locomotive was the '2251' class 0–6–0 which was a taper-boilered version of the celebrated 'Dean Goods', and on this account could equally well be referred to as a Dean derivative.

The South Wales tank, of the '5600' class, was a new design from the machinery point of view, though using the standard No 2 taper boiler. This new design, of which the first order was for fifty, was to work alongside, and eventually to replace, the various designs of 0–6–2 tank operating on the local railways. The standard Great Western wheel diameter of 4ft 7½in was used, but otherwise the 'engine' and framing were new. The late A. W. J. Dymond, who was originally a 'Taff' man, told me once how very seriously the designing work was taken at Swindon. Under Hawksworth's guidance he did much of

117

the work, and he recalled to me how Hawksworth repeatedly emphasised to him: 'There's no prototype; we're in for fifty'. The wheelbase of these engines was the same as that of the Rhymney 0–6–2 tanks, and the 'R' and 'M' class engines of the latter railway, in their turn, were fitted with the Great Western No 2 Standard taper boiler. The '56XX' class had cylinders 18in diameter by 26in stroke, with direct Stephenson link motion, and with boilers carrying a pressure of 200lb per square inch their nominal tractive effort was 25,800lb. Eventually their numbers were increased to a total of 200, the running numbers being 5600 to 5699, and 6600 to 6699.

There is no doubt that Swindon would have liked to use the standard No 2 boiler on all the South Wales tank engines that had a good working life remaining; but for most of them the barrel was too long, and so, while using all existing flanging plates and tools, a shorter version of the S2 was designed. This was intermediate between the S2 and the still smaller variety used on the '45XX' 2–6–2 tanks. A still further new variety was prepared to suit the Taff Vale '04' class engines, known as the S3, which could best be described as having an S10 barrel with an S2 firebox. The principal dimensions of these three classes of boiler fitted to ex-South Wales railways locomotives are shown in Table 18.

TABLE 18

SOUTH WALES TANK ENGINES: GWR BOILERS

Boiler Designation		S2	S3	S10
Barrel dia min		$4-5\frac{1}{8}$	$4-5\frac{1}{8}$	$4-5\frac{1}{8}$
dia max		$5-0\frac{1}{2}$	$5-0\frac{1}{2}$	$5-0\frac{1}{2}$
length		11–0	10–3	10–3
Total evaporative heating surface	sq ft	1349	1267	1248
Superheater	sq ft	82.2	76	76
Grate area	sq ft	20.35	20.35	17.4
Working pressure	psi	200	175	200*

*Some engines had a reduced boiler pressure of 175lb per sq in

These three standard boilers covered a considerable number of Taff Vale, Rhymney, Cardiff, and Brecon & Merthyr tank engines and the S10 was used on two new Great Western classes to be described in due course. On the Barry Railway two of John Auld's 0–6–4 tank engines received No 4 standard boiler, as used on the 'Cities', 'Counties' and the '42XX' 2–8–0 tanks; but these two locomotives did not long survive in their rebuilt form. The S10 boiler was used on the taper-boilered version of the 'Dean Goods' produced in 1930. This had the same chassis and engine layout, but with a boiler pressure of 200lb per square inch against 180 the nominal tractive effort was increased from 18,140 to 20,155lb. The total weight of the engine alone in working order was 43 tons against 36.8, and the maximum axle-load went up from 13 tons to 15¾ tons. They proved smart little engines and did much good work.

I come next to the important group of locomotives derived from the 'Saint' class 4–6–0. In the original scheme of locomotive standardisation, as represented by a diagram dated 1901, Churchward included a 4–6–0 with coupled wheels 5ft 8½in diameter, and using the same boiler as the express passenger 4–6–0 and the freight 2–8–0. At that time there was a very clear-cut line of demarcation in the working of the West of England traffic at Newton Abbot. In broad gauge days the 8ft singles had never worked west of Newton, and this tradition continued in early standard gauge days, with the Dean 7ft 8in singles working own from Paddington or Bristol, and the 'Duke' class 4–4–0s carrying on to Plymouth and in Cornwall. The construction of the 5ft 8½in 'Bulldog' class 4–4–0s followed the same precepts. But the development of the very powerful Churchward 4–6–0s, and the collateral development of train services, with reduction of loads on the heaviest trains by the detaching of slip portions, tended to even out the demands upon locomotives. The loads were reduced as the gradients became progressively more severe. Furthermore, the keen desire of the high management to establish record lengths of daily non-stop run indicated Plymouth as a much more suitable engine-changing point than Newton Abbot. It was found that with the reduced loads the express passenger 4–6–0s could take the South Devon banks in their stride, and the need for the projected 4–6–0 with 5ft 8½in wheels did not eventuate.

In the 1920s however, the physical conditions on so much of the line that had justified the building of large numbers of

'Bulldogs' twenty years earlier, demanded the introduction of a much more powerful general service locomotive. The standard two-cylinder 'engine', with its very effective setting of the Stephenson link motion provided an ideal basis, but in planning a general service unit a wheel diameter of 6ft 0in was chosen, instead of Churchward's original 5ft 8½in No 2925 *Saint Martin* was rebuilt, in 1925, with 6ft diameter coupled wheels. The tractive effort was increased from 24,395lb to 27,272lb; but apart from the reduction in coupled wheel diameter the only alteration was to fit the Collett type of cab, which at that time had been confined to the 'Castle' class engines. The rebuilt *Saint Martin* had the original type of tender, as normally attached to all the larger Churchward tender engines at that time. *Saint Martin* remained a prototype for nearly three years and as it proved successful authority was given for construction of no fewer than eighty new engines of the same type, as a replacement for the various 6ft 8½in 4-4-0s, and eventually of other classes. So in 1928 came the celebrated '49XX', or 'Hall' class. Having had 'Cities' and 'Counties', and then followed up with 'Courts', 'Abbeys' and 'Castles', it was perhaps natural to turn to a slightly lesser strata among the stately homes of England for names. All the same, when the first authorisation was for *eighty* engines of this new class a systematised form of nomenclature had its problems—especially as many more were envisaged, even from the start. Nevertheless, after an abortive but highly amusing start in the search for names on the part of the locomotive drawing office, a more general survey showed there was no lack of 'Halls' after which engines might be named; and it was only after the class had topped the 200 mark that the search extended to Yorkshire and the Lake District.

Names apart however, the 'Hall' class locomotives, except for a few superficial details such as cabs, were pure Churchward. They were extremely strong and reliable at low speeds and ran freely up to about 75mph. In the GWR engine lists they were designated 'Passenger' but their high tractive effort at low and medium speeds led to their regular use on heavy mixed traffic and fast freight services. Their introduction on to the Birmingham–Bristol route gave an excellent opportunity for their work to be studied through the recordings of several experienced observers who regularly logged the running of the 'Penzance', between Stratford-on-Avon and Birmingham. Coming at the end of a long working, it was not only a test of actual performance, but also a measure of how things had been maintained earlier, and whether the firebox conditions were favourable in the concluding stages of a long run. The salient details of five runs on this train with loads varying between 345 and 410 tons are given in Table 19, and the first point that will be noted is that on no one occasion was there any time to spare. It would have made a great deal of difference if the train could have run fast in from Hall Green; but there was not only the very severe slack through Tyseley, but often a subsequent slack to cross over from one set of tracks to the other.

In the accompanying table I have shown not only the running times and speeds, but have also made estimates of the sustained drawbar horsepower on the long bank, and of the rate of evaporation in the boiler. The latter figures are important because in the tests carried out on 'Hall' class locomotives in British Railways days the maximum continuous rate of evaporation in the boiler was assessed at about 23,000lb per hour. The Henley bank is too long to practice the mortgaging technique to any extent, and the performance normally reflected continuous output standards. In climbing the bank speed had normally fallen to a sustained minimum figure by Wood End Halt, on the 1 in 150 gradient, and some acceleration would be noted on the last 2 miles at 1 in 181 up to Earlswood Lakes. The second run with *Gatacre Hall* and a 350-ton load showed the highest horsepower, but the highest drawbar pull goes to the credit of *Shirenewton Hall* on the fifth run. When we come to estimating the rate of evaporation, runs 1, 3, 4 and 5 show values of 20,000 to 21,000lb per hour, and the finest of them all, No 2, was not far short of the boiler limit. It is remarkable that such efforts could be obtained from the engines at the concluding end of a long run. The relation of drawbar pull to the nominal tractive effort is interesting. The general average of this ratio is 30 to 34 per cent, and represents a comfortable optimum performance rather than an all-out maximum. The phenomenal effort of *Stanford Court* referred to in Chapter 4, which

TABLE 19

HALL CLASS PERFORMANCE: HENLEY BANK

Run No	1	2	3	4	5
Engine No	4928	4928	4929	4928	4967
Engine Name	*Gatacre Hall*	*Gatacre Hall*	*Goytrey Hall*	*Gatacre Hall*	*Shirenewton Hall*
Load tons E/F	327/345	332/350	359/385	382/410	384/410
Distance	Actual	Actual	Actual	Actual	Actual
Miles	min sec	min sec	min sec	min sec	min sec
0.0 STRATFORD-ON-AVON	0 00	0 00	0 00	0 00	0 00
5.5 *Milepost 16*	8 50	8 54	8 22	9 09	9 10
8.0 HENLEY-IN-ARDEN	11 37	11 34	11 00	11 45	11 48
12.8 Wood End	17 33	17 22	17 15	18 00	18 01
14.8 Earlswood Lakes	20 01	19 43	19 54	20 47	20 45
—				—	pws
21.7 Tyseley	26 50	26 43	26 47	27 42	30 27
—			sigs	—	—
25.0 BIRMINGHAM	32 20	32 42	33 02	32 22	35 20
Speeds: mph					
Milepost 16	56	58	62	60	61
Wood End	47	48	42½	42½	42
Earlswood Lakes	48½	51½	46	43	44½
Evaporation lb/hr	20,000	22,000	20,500	20,000	21,000
DHP at Earlswood	1055	1155	1080	1050	1095
Drawbar Pull lb	8230	8400	8850	9200	9250
Ratio: *DB Pull* % *Nom. TE*	30	30.7	32.3	33.7	34.0

yielded a drawbar pull of more than 7 tons at 30mph, represented an output of nearly 68 per cent of the nominal tractive effort—the highest I have ever seen with a British locomotive.

The 'Halls' proved a splendid investment, and this work on the North Warwick line gives an excellent guide to the way they performed on other hilly routes. As to their high speed capabilities, a run I logged from Reading to Paddington with one of the Weymouth trains gives a good indication. The load was no more than light, totalling only 235 tons gross behind the tender, but until a bad signal check came at Hayes the engine ran very freely. Twyford, 5 miles, was passed in 7min 10sec at 65mph and speed was continuously at 73-75mph from Maidenhead to Slough. There was a slight falling off afterwards, but Milepost $11\frac{1}{2}$, 24.5 miles from the start was passed in $23\frac{1}{2}$min. The check at Hayes compelled a reduction of speed to 20mph but speed was worked up rapidly afterwards, and Paddington, 36 miles, reached in 38min 20sec, despite the check. The net time for this smart run was 35min. The engine was No 5949 *Trematon Hall*, about which I have another story to tell shortly.

While the 'Hall' class locomotives took over certain duties previously worked by the 'Saints' the engines of this latter class that were being withdrawn were officially replaced by new 'Castles'. In 1936 the time had come for some of the earliest units of the '43XX' class of 2-6-0 to be replaced, and it was then that the 5ft $8\frac{1}{2}$in 4-6-0 proposed by Churchward in 1901 actually materialised, as the new 'Grange' class. Like the 'Halls' these new engines were pure-Churchward, in having the standard two-cylinder 'engine' layout, and the No 1 standard boiler. Because of the still smaller coupled wheels the nominal tractive effort was further increased to 28,875lb. There were eventually eighty engines of this class and as with the 'Halls' there was a pretty thorough search round Great Western territory for names of stately homes. One must be pardoned for wondering if the same edifice did not appear under two different designations, as for example, the new *Arlington Grange* and the veteran *Arlington Court*, *Broughton Grange* and *Broughton Hall*—not to mention *Broughton Castle!*—*Highnam Court* and *Highnam Grange*. I always remember too, the novice among Great Western admirers who once got seriously perplexed as to whether *Saint Benet's Hall*, *Saint Bride's Hall* and *Saint Edmund Hall* belonged to the 'Saint' or the 'Hall' class. Joking apart, however, those responsible for choosing the names for these numerous mixed traffic units did their job remarkably well. In the late summer of 1971 I was in Canada, and attended a Steam Rally at Milton near Toronto, which included a $3\frac{1}{2}$-inch gauge circuit for 'live steamers'. Among various Canadian and American types there were several models of British prototypes. These beautiful little engines worked well, and pulled loads of delighted children and adults. Then fairly late in the day yet another Canadian participant arrived, with a truly exquisite model of GWR No 5949; but he had evidently considered that the name of the Cornish stately home would have little or no significance in Ontario, so he had renamed his engine *Lickham Hall*: and by her immaculate performance round that circuit she very nearly did!

The 'Granges' as might be expected, were excellent mixed traffic engines, and at summer holiday weekends were frequently called upon to take many passenger trains. Although it is taking the story forward into British Railways times, one of the finest runs I have ever seen with one of these engines came when the 'Britannia' class 4-6-2 working the 12.20pm up from Cardiff failed, and had to come off the train at Swindon. Engine No 6832 *Brockton Grange* was commandered at a moment's notice, and took over the haulage of a heavy train totalling 485 tons, gross behind the tender. The driver started away gently, while he was taking the measure of the locomotive and his mate was getting the fire into shape for a big effort. So they took $14\frac{1}{2}$min to cover the first 10.8 miles, to Uffington. By then, however, the engine was going in first class style at $67\frac{1}{2}$mph and then they ran continuously at 70-74mph until slowing for permanent way repairs near Pangbourne. After that there were several checks and the engine was not worked so vigorously. But despite a dead stand for signals at Taplow the run of 77.3 miles from Swindon to Paddington was completed in $84\frac{1}{4}$min and the net time did not exceed 80min. For a 'scratch' engine, picked at a moment's notice this was a particularly good effort with a train of 485 tons.

The last of the 4–6–0 derivatives were the lightweight 'Manors' of 1938. These engines were also designed as a replacement for the '43XX' 2–6–0s, and they had the same wheel spacing as the 'Granges'. Although having the standard 2-cylinder engine layout the cylinders were 18in diameter instead of 18½in, and the nominal tractive effort was reduced to 27,340lb. In order to keep the weight down the boiler had to be much smaller. It was shorter, smaller in its diameters, and had a smaller grate. The comparative dimensions are shown in Table 20.

TABLE 20

Class	'Grange'	'Manor'
Heating surface sq ft		
Tubes	1686.60	1285.5
Firebox	154.78	140
Superheater	262.62	160
Grate Area sq ft	27.07	22.1

Even taking the most charitable view of it, however, the 'Manor' as originally built was not a successful design. Looking back in retrospect it seems extraordinary that Swindon having produced such a dynasty of excellent boilers should, in 1938, have suddenly introduced one that was such a poor steamer. In any case a study of the heating surfaces alone in relation to those of the standard No 1 suggest that the 'Manor' was very much 'under-boilered' in relation to its high nominal tractive effort. But much worse than this was the fact that the evaporative performance of the boiler did not correspond even to the reduced heating surfaces and grate area. Except in its very small superheater the 'Manor' boiler could be described as roughly 75 per cent of that of a 'Grange', but whereas the latter could be relied upon to produce between 20,000 and 22,000lb of steam per hour, that of the 'Manor' could do no better than 10,000lb. This very serious deficiency, it should be explained, was not revealed in full quantitative form until an important series of tests was carried out at Swindon in 1951-2. All that was known in the early days was that the 'Manors' were not very free in steaming.

In view of what was subsequently found the reason was not difficult to establish. The boiler itself and the firebox

were designed on well-established Swindon practice. But—
and one hesitates to criticise without knowing all the facts of
what transpired in the drawing office at the time—sadly in-
sufficient attention seems to have been given to the draughting. Here was a potentially powerful locomotive, required
for a road with some very heavy gradients, but where the civil
engineering restrictions demanded the use of a boiler only
some three-quarters of the size that would ordinarily have
been provided. One would have thought that particular attention would have been given to making that small boiler steam
with the utmost freedom. Instead all that was done was to
take the standard blastpipe and jumper top, as used with the
No 1 boiler, and reduce the orifice from $5\frac{1}{4}$in to $5\frac{1}{8}$in—a reduction in area to no more than 95 per cent of the No 1
standard. The jumper top, when lifted, increased the area by
some 40 per cent so that one derived no extra benefit in
draughting by trying to work the engine 'heavy'. The 'Manors'
were designed specially for the Cambrian section, where the
principal haulage problem was set by the notorious Talerddig bank, with its many miles of 1 in 52 ascent. I had a number of runs with these engines, and my impression always was
that they were being treated gently, even the loads they took
unassisted on the banks were usually well below 300 tons.

Only twenty of these locomotives had been built by the end
of World War I, but as indicating most forcefully where the
deficiency in their design lay I must add that prior to the important series of trials carried out on engine No 7818 in
1951-2, the draughting arrangements had been modified, according to the principles established in the locomotive testing
section of the Western Region. A plain-topped blastpipe with
an orifice diameter of $4\frac{5}{8}$in had been substituted for the
jumper top. The chimney itself was also redesigned. As a result of these changes which, it will be appreciated, reduced
the area of the orifice to 77 per cent of that of the No 1—in
almost exact proportion to the reduction in heating surface
and grate area—the performance of the boiler was transformed. Evaporation rates of the order of 20,000lb per hour
were obtained, even with coal of lower grades, though in this,
of course, the absence of the jumper ring eliminated the enlargement of the orifice when the engine was working heavy',

and resulted in a very sharp exhaust through the simple blast-pipe top. The alteration to the draughting of the 'Manor' class engines in British Railways was only one point in the modernisation of Swindon designs to suit the post-war conditions. The changes made to the 'Hall' class by Mr Hawksworth, are discussed later.

Turning now to the standard outside-cylindered tank engines, the Great Western entered the grouping era with four well-established classes. There were the three 'large' types: the '22XX' class 4–4–2, the '31XX' class 2–6–2 and the '42XX' class 2–8–0. The first named had 18in by 30in cylinders, and the No 2 standard boiler; the other two classes had 18½in cylinders and the No 4 boiler. The speedworthiness of the standard locomotives with 5ft 8in coupled wheels was found to provide everything in the way of fast running that was needed in shorter distance passenger train working, and so the '22XX', or 'County tanks', became obsolete. To replace these engines, and also to provide a more powerful unit to replace the various Dean six-wheeled tank engines and the '36XX' class 2–4–2 tanks, the '51XX' class was introduced. This was a synthesis of existing components having the chassis and wheels of the heavy '31XX' 2–6–2 tank, but the smaller No 2 standard boiler and 18in diameter cylinders. By comparison with the '31XX' class, the '51XX' had a maximum axle load of 17.6 tons, against 19.25, and the nominal tractive effort was 24,300lb against 25,670lb. This class was introduced in 1929, and quickly became the standard suburban tank engine in all the busy districts. One hundred of these engines were built, numbered from 5100 to 5199, and these were followed by a further hundred, Nos 6100-6199 with boilers carrying a pressure of 225lb per square inch. These had an increased nominal tractive effort of 27,340lb. A further forty locomotives of the '51XX' class were built, carrying numbers 4100 to 4139.

A curious experiment was made with two series of 2–6–2 tanks, using coupled wheels smaller than the standard 5ft 8in diameter. Five engines of the 'heavy' '31XX' were rebuilt with 5ft 3in coupled wheels, and ten of the '61XX' class were built new with 5ft 6in wheels and numbered 8100 to 8109. In view of the criticism that followed the departure from the standard 6ft 8in wheels to 6ft 6in for the 'Kings', and the costs involved in making new patterns, one is curious to know why so small a change in diameter should have been decided upon for the '61XX' class. They can have made little if any difference to the performance. In the case of the five '31XX' engines one would imagine that the 5ft 3in wheels were the 5ft 2in standard on the Dean goods and the '2251' class 0-6-0, but with thicker tyres; but there again, why not use 5ft 2in, if a diameter of that order was desired. As a result of these variations the GWR had, by the end of the 1930s, five varieties of large 2-6-2 tank as shown in Table 21.

TABLE 21

2-6-2 TANK VARIETIES

Series	Cylinder dia	Coupled wheel dia	Boiler pressure	Nom. T.E.	No of engs
	in	ft in	psi	lb	
3150	18½	5-8	200	25,670	41
3100	18½	5-3	225	31,170	5
5100	18	5-8	200	24,300	140
6100	18	5-8	225	27,340	100
8100	18	5-6	225	28,165	10

The Churchward 2-8-0 tanks of the '42XX' class introduced in 1910 for short-haul workings with heavy coal trains in South Wales, had proved very successful and by 1930 mustered a total of 219 engines. But the gradual withdrawal of the inside-cylindered 'Aberdare' class 2-6-0s called for some replacement, despite the falling off of traffic, and in 1934 twenty locomotives of the '42XX' class were converted into 2-8-2 tanks, by enlarging the coal bunker and the tanks, and adding a pair of trailing wheels. The tank capacity was increased from 1,800 to 2,500 gallons, and the bunkers henceforth took no less than 6 tons of coal. They were then able to undertake main line freight train workings of an intermediate character, running from South Wales to Salisbury, for example. Altogether fifty-four of these locomotives were converted from 2-8-0s and took the running numbers 7200-7253.

Although it could not be described as a 'derivative' from

Page 129. (above) *4–4–0 No 3828* County of Hereford; (below) *Up Weymouth express near Acton, engine No 3807* County Kilkenny

Page 130. (above) *4–4–0 No 4120* Atbara; (centre) *2–4–2 tank engine No 3626;* (below) *'Bulldog' class 4–4–0 No 3338* Swift

Churchward practice, in that it was one of his own designs, I cannot conclude this chapter without making some reference to those splendid engines, the '45XX' class of 2–6–2 tank. I have referred in Chapter 1 to the work they were doing in 1922. Their numbers were subsequently increased until there was a total of 175, and they were in use on light duties all over the system. I trust, however, that I shall be forgiven for adding that I have always thought they were ugly engines. The Churchward standard features were all present in them, but the low pitch of their small taper boiler, and their tall cabs gave them an odd, unbalanced look, which was not present in the larger engines on which the boiler centre-line was higher. Churchward himself was not one to mind very much what his engines looked like, so long as they did their job. And although in response to some good-natured badinage from James Stirling he had greatly improved the appearance of the 'Saint' class 4–6–0s one can quite well imagine he could not have been bothered about so secondary a class as the light branch line tank.

While they were familiar objects to me on most parts of the GWR system my most vivid memory of them will always be of a short, totally unexpected run on the Bristol main line. At one time my usual homeward train from Chippenham to Bath was the 4.15pm from Paddington, which called conveniently at Chippenham at 6.20pm, and having a buffet car gave the opportunity of a 'noggin' of some kind in the short run to Bath. The train was a return working for Bristol men of the 11.45am up non-stop from Temple Meads to Paddington; the engine was nearly always a 'Castle', but occasionally one of the post-war '1000' class 'Counties'. One day the train arrived at Chippenham on time, but with the engine a complete failure! It was a 'County' and one of the valve rods had fractured. There was a '45XX' class 2–6–2 tank waiting on the bay road ready to take the stopping train, and with the utmost promptitude this engine was taken to tow off the disabled 'County', park it, and then couple on to the express. The little engine was no real match for an eleven coach corridor train, but she was flailed without mercy, and we climbed the 1 in 660 to Corsham to the accompaniment of a terrific tattoo from the exhaust. Once into Box Tunnel the little

131

engine was eased down, and speed did not exceed 52mph but we reached Bath, 12.7 miles in just over 18min. Driver W. Brown, of Bath Road shed, was a top link man whom I got to know well in later years, and rode several times with on the footplate. He told me of an amusing sequal when they reached Bristol. The engine was bunker first, and a platform inspector seeing them run in was horrified. He hurried up to him, and asked why the blue-pencil they had not taken the trouble to turn the engine round before they started! Having witnessed with admiration the speed with which the substitution of engines had taken place at Chippenham, and the train restarted less than twenty minutes late I can well imagine that Bill Brown and his mate had a very appropriate reply to that platform inspector!

CHAPTER 9

Derivatives from Dean Designs

IN writing of the period 1923 to 1948 it might seem passing strange that any new designs should have been derived from the work of an engineer whose career lay almost entirely in the nineteenth century. It is true that he did not actually retire till 1902, and that a number of important developments took place at Swindon in the last years of his chieftainship; but it is equally well known today that these new developments were the work of Churchward and that Dean's influence had begun to wane even by the time of the building of the 'Badminton' class locomotives. At the time of the grouping, however, the Great Western had on its very active locomotive list a matter of 1,100 tank engines of the 0-6-0 type, for all of which there were important if humdrum jobs; and before very long many of these engines would have to be replaced. They were literally of all shapes and sizes, and used for shunting, branch line passenger, auto-train working and light goods. There were side tanks, saddle-tanks, and panniers of every vintage, and while 2-4-0s like the gallant little 'Metropolitans' were down to be replaced by powerful 2-6-2 tanks, the swarm of little engines on more humdrum duties was simply crying out for rationalisation. The fact that they had survived throughout the Churchward era when standardisation was so very much in the air is a measure of their inherent soundness of design, and of the good state of repair in which they had been maintained.

One factor that directly, or indirectly, must have profoundly influenced the decisions that were taken concerning the replacement of the older six-wheeled tank engines was the existence, still in first-rate fettle, of the 'Dean Goods' 0-6-0s. While this design had originated in the Dean era, and was some forty years old at the time of grouping, the modifications that had been made to it subsequently in the fitting of super-heated boilers and Belpaire fireboxes put the class in much the same category as the so-called 'Ivatt' large-boilered 'Atlantics' on the Great Northern Railway. Both locomotive classes were subjected to highly important improvements by the respective successors of the engineers whose names they ordinarily carried. At the same time one feels that the influence of the 'Dean Goods', or the 'Dean-Churchward Goods' as it should more correctly be designated, was indirect. Although its continuing prowess was well appreciated at Swindon there can have been few—in the 1923-45 era at any rate—who appreciated how good, by how much in advance of the times the design really was. In a book like this it is difficult, even if it were desirable, to preserve strict chronological order. To follow up these comments about the 'Dean Goods' I am once again stepping forward to the time just after nationalisation of British Railways in 1948. It will be readily appreciated that the new management would be inclined to be disparaging about a design of 0–6–0 tender engine that was of strongly Victorian appearance, and which was then some sixty years old. Consideration was given to the replacement of the veterans by a modern design lately brought out by the LMS, and including, in popular parlance, 'all mod cons' in the form of self-cleaning smokeboxes, rocking grates, roller bearing axle boxes and a commodious cab, designed to give protection to the enginemen equally in both directions of running. This, of course, was the Ivatt class '2' of the '6400' class. Its tractive effort was a little less than that of the old GWR 0–6–0—17,400 lb against 18,140lb—but in the first place it was assumed that the improved characteristics of the modern design would yield so improved a performance that the reduced tractive effort would not matter.

The new LMS 2–6–0 was tested with the dynamometer car between Crewe and Holyhead, and no doubt had been expressed about the locomotives being able to do the work for which they had been designed. But when the question arose as to their being used as a replacement for the 'Dean Goods' several points arose. First of all, the new class '2' had been designed to work on hard coal, and on Western Region duties there would be times when it would have to work on soft Welsh coal, and coal moreover of a quality below that used for the important main line duties. The first experiences with the class '2' on Western Region work, both passenger and goods, were so unsatisfactory as to cause some concern. The new engine did not appear capable of undertaking tasks that the old 'Dean Goods' was performing with complete success. Accordingly, a series of tests on the stationary plant at Swindon was arranged. It was soon evident that the class '2' would not steam on Welsh coal, and to enable tests to be made the blast pipe cap had the orifice reduced to $3\frac{7}{8}$in diameter. Even though the rate of steam production was increased it was still appreciably less than that of the 'Dean Goods'. I think it fair to say that the performance of this old 0–6–0, analysed fundamentally for the first time on the Swindon stationary plant, surprised even the Western Region pundits. And when the news got around that a 60-year-old Great Western 0–6–0 had, on test, licked the proverbial pants off a brand new LMS 2–6–0 there was joy abounding among the devotees of Swindon and everything that emerged from it.

This episode, highly gratifying as it was to all Great Western supporters, was of far greater importance historically than a victory for Swindon in the Inter-Regional 'power game' that developed after nationalisation. The tests of the two locomotives provided a complete thermodynamic record of the performance of the old 0–6–0, and constituted a record of working of by far the oldest locomotive ever subjected to such modern, scientific analysis. It arose out of the fact that the LMS 2–6–0 as received at Swindon could not work the loads laid down for Group 'A' locomotives on gradients steeper than 1 in 70. There were plenty of gradients of that severity where the 'Dean Goods' engines were then working, and a great deal of hard work on the part of the testing staff of the Western Region was devoted to trying to bring the steaming and haulage capacity of the LMS 2–6–0 up to the standard of the old 0–6–0. They very nearly, but not quite, achieved this; but although they transformed a poor steaming engine into a reliable unit, on the coals supplied for the arduous duties laid down, the 'Dean Goods' still very slightly had the advantage over the rival in the higher ranges of the power output scales.

TABLE 22

EVAPORATION RESULTS
'Dean Goods' : 2301 class

Coal fired lb per hour	Evaporation lb per hour	
	Bedwas coal	Blidworth coal
600	6000	5000
800	7700	6700
1000	9100	8000
1200	10400	9400
1400	11600	10500
1600	12500	11500
1800	13100	12200
2000	13700	13000
2200	—	13700
Calorific value of coal BThU/lb	14000	12820

Blidworth coal is the well-known 'hard' East Midlands, graded as 2B, while Bedwas, also of Grade 2B, is a rather friable Welsh type. When dry both had much the same calorific value, but the Blidworth coal, as received for locomotive use, had a high moisture content which reduced its effectiveness to the value shown in the table. In passing one may comment that an output of 13,700lb of steam per hour was remarkable to obtain from a boiler with a combined heating surface of 1,142.6sq ft and a grate area of 15.45sq ft. The corresponding evaporation figures for the LMS class '2' were a maximum of 12,000lb per hour on Bedwas coal, requiring 2,000lb of coal per hour, while on Blidworth the 'Dean Goods' maximum of 13,700lb per hour was equalled, but only when the firing rate was stepped up to 2,600lb per hour.

The influence of the 'Dean Goods' on the steam locomotive practice of the nationalised British Railways was not finished with the great improvements made to the LMS class '2' 2-6-0, which of course formed the basis of a British Standard design. The data obtained from the steaming tests on the Swindon stationary testing plant had created a deep impression upon the engineers concerned. It was something to be remembered, and although the primary task was to find means of improving the LMS 2–6–0 it could not be otherwise than a matter of intense pride among ex-Great Western men that it was the 'Dean Goods' that had helped them to do it. When the Harrow disaster in 1952 had resulted, among other things, in the almost complete destruction of the 'Pacific' locomotive *Princess Anne*, the decision had been taken to replace this with a prototype class '8' express passenger Pacific in the British Railways standard stud. This was specified as a three-cylinder engine with Caprotti valve gear, and as usual with the British Standard locomotives the design was divided between several of the major drawing offices. So while Derby was the parent office, Swindon was given the task of designing the draughting, among other items. As is well known, the resulting locomotive, No 71000, had a twin-orifice blastpipe and double-chimney. What is perhaps not so widely known is that the blastpipe dimensions and chimney were precisely those of a 'Dean Goods'—two '2301' blastpipes side by side!

I must now revert to the Collett era, when the sterling worth of the modernised 'Dean Goods' with superheater boilers was known, and largely taken for granted. Since grouping the passenger work on the former Cambrian Railways had been largely performed by the 'Duke' class 4–4–0s, another excellent Dean design, that dated from 1895. A start had been made with the fitting of boilers with Belpaire fireboxes from 1901 onwards and with superheating from 1912. But in the 1930s these engines were ageing, and replacement had to be considered. An obvious answer would have been to substitute the 'Bulldog' class 4–4–0s, many of which were being replaced by the new mixed-traffic engines of the 'Hall' class. But the 'Bulldogs', with a maximum load of 17.6 tons were too heavy for the Cambrian line, and so a compromise was made by rebuilding twenty engines of this class with parallel domed boilers, generally the same as used hitherto on the 'Duke' class. There were several varieties of boiler on the latter class, including some that were still non-superheated; but the rebuilt engines, originally numbered in the '3200' series, had smaller superheaters than those of the 'Dukes'. Both in the barrel and the firebox these boilers were larger than those of the 'Dean Goods'. The leading dimensions of both are given in Table 23.

TABLE 23

BOILERS OF DEAN DERIVATIVES

Class	'2301'	'3200'
Barrel, length	10ft 3in	11ft 0in
Outside diameter max	4ft 5in	4ft 5in
min	4ft 4in	4ft 4in
Heating surfaces:		
Tubes	960.85sq ft	1028.95sq ft
Firebox	106.45sq ft	113.95sq ft
Superheater	75.3sq ft	75.3sq ft
Grate Area	15.45sq ft	17.2sq ft
Boiler pressure	180psi	180psi

The rebuilt engines of the '3200' had the same cylinders, coupled wheels, and frames as the 'Bulldogs', but the tractive effort was 18,955lb against 21,060lb on account of a lower working pressure. The maximum axle load of the rebuilds was 15.4 tons, against 17.6 tons, and this made them acceptable for the Cambrian section.

The 'Duke' class engines were all named, but although the majority of their titles had some association with the West Country they were a miscellaneous lot savouring more of the Crewe style of nomenclature rather than of the systematised practice of Swindon. The rebuilt engines of the '3200' class were at first being named after Earls, mostly titles of directors or other eminent men associated with the Great Western Railway. The naming of these engines was however not taken as the honour that was intended by some of the personalities concerned, and it was intimated that to place the names upon locomotives of such secondary importance was hardly in keeping with the dignity of the titles concerned. So after thirteen engines had been built the names were transferred to the 5043 to 5055 batch of 'Castles'. Further engines of the class were nameless from the start. Until then they had been known as the 'Earl' class, but in due course the English genius for coining nicknames came to the fore and in recognition of the dual parentage of the locomotives some 'wag' coined the name 'Dukedogs'! In later years, when it was desired to number additional engines of the '2251' class of 0-6-0s in the '3200' range, the 'Dukedogs' were renumbered 9000 to 9029. The '3200' class engines that at one time carried names were:

3200	*Earl of Mount Edgecumbe*
3201	*Earl of Dunraven*
3202	*Earl of Dudley*
3203	*Earl Cawdor*
3204	*Earl of Dartmouth*
3205	*Earl of Devon*
3206	*Earl of Plymouth*
3207	*Earl of St Germans*
3208	*Earl Bathurst*
3209	*Earl of Radnor*
3210	*Earl Cairns*
3211	*Earl of Ducie*
3212	*Earl of Eldon*

The names originally selected for the remaining engines of the first batch of 'Earls' were put on to the 'Castles' 5056 to 5062.

They were excellent engines in their own particular range of power. I had some footplate journeys with them on the Cambrian line, and they worked efficiently and very smoothly on that heavily graded route. Unfortunately I did not get the opportunity to test the unaided capacity of one of them in climbing the Talerddig bank, for we had a load that was beyond the limit for one engine—seven coaches of 221 tons tare. We took the assistance of a '45XX' 2-6-2 tank engine from Machynlleth up to Talerddig, and the 'Dukedog' did not require to be worked harder than 25 per cent cut-off for the speed to be held at 28 to 29mph on the 1 in 50 gradient. On the continuation to Welshpool on gradients favourable at first but undulating afterwards engine No 9027 did well. She was driven and fired in the traditional Great Western style keeping boiler pressure up to 'sizzling' point, without allowing the valve to blow off fully, and working in 25 per cent cut-off and a varied regulator opening, as on the Churchward two-cylinder locomotives. She ran very smoothly, and although having coupled wheels no larger than 5ft 8½in diameter she ran freely at speeds up to 60 and 65mph between stops.

Although larger engines in the form of the 'Manor' class 4–6–0s were introduced on to this route, the 'Dukedogs' were in regular use well into the 1950s.

In 1929 replacement began of the large stud of six-wheeled tank engines. It would be impossible within the confines of a single chapter to attempt even a broad summary of the multitude of existing locomotives. The most important group, many of which survived to enter British Railways' stock, were the 0–6–0 pannier tanks. Six broad varieties may be mentioned, all of nineteenth-century vintage, and all, one suspects, the result of the continuing powerful influence of George Armstrong at Wolverhampton Works. In Dean's time Wolverhampton enjoyed a degree of marked autonomy, not only in the management of its workshops but in the design of locomotives. Some of these classes had begun their existence as saddle tanks, but in the early grouping days all had been modernised and their tank capacity increased.

TABLE 24

EARLY PANNIER TANK 0–6–0s

Class	Date	Cylinders in diameter	stroke	Coupled wheel diameter ft in	Boiler pressure psi	No in service 1947
'1501'	1878	17	24	4–7½	165	12
'1701'	1891	17	24	4–7½	180	38
'1813'	1882	17	24	4–7½	165	1
'1901'	1891	16	24	4–1½	165	43
'2021'	1897	16½	24	4–1½	165	110
'2700'	1896	17½	24	4–7½	180	60

The numbers of these veterans still existing in 1947 is quoted in Table 24 to indicate those that passed into British Railways stock, despite the substantial replacements that had taken place since 1929. In all, a total of 370 saddle or pannier tank 0–6–0s had been built between 1891 and 1905, 160 at Swindon and 210 at Wolverhampton, and most of these were in service in 1929. The '2021' class was then 140 strong, and of the '2700' class there were the 100 originally built. Some of the earlier engines had outside frames, but the '1813' and '1901' classes with inside frames were instantly recognisable as the progenitors of the Collett replacements of 1929. The '1901' class was still considered a Great Western 'standard' at the end of World War II, for light branch and shunting work, and its dimensions, alongside those of the new '6400' and '5700' classes, are set out in Table 26. There were 123 of the '1901' class in service in 1929.

While it might seem that the new engines of 1929 were little more than a straight continuation of the '2700' class with higher boiler pressure, they did have a number of improvements, particularly in respect of the valve setting. They were extremely powerful and free-running locomotives, and I shall never forget the comment of a Welsh driver: 'They're *dynamic*!' By the time the Great Western Railway passed into national ownership no fewer than 853 of these splendid engines were in service, together with some 200 remaining of the older classes. The numbers of the new '5700' class ran as follows: 3600 to 3799; 4600 to 4699; 5700 to 5799; 6700 to 6799; 7700 to 7799; 8700 to 8799; 9600 to 9682; 9700 to 9799.

Many stories could be told about the versatility of these engines. At one time there used to be a stopping train from Bath to Chippenham that followed the old 7.45am express from Bristol to Paddington. I used the 'stopper' on many occasions, and it was frequently worked by a '5700' class 0–6–0. 'Dynamic' was certainly the word! It was on the 4½-mile run downhill at 1 in 660 between Corsham and Chippenham that those engines used really to get going, and with a load of two or three bogie coaches the speed frequently topped the 60mph mark before steam was shut off. There were three drivers in this particular link, and on one memorable morning the most enterprising of the three had a special opportunity to show his prowess. The 'Castle' working the preceeding London express arrived in Bath with a broken tender axlebox spring, and had to come off the train. Bath fortunately had a 'Bulldog' class 4–4–0 near at hand, but this was not adequate to take a 450-ton train up through Box Tunnel, so the pannier tank waiting to take the stopper was attached as pilot. The driver really worked her hard, to the amazement and delight of the Old Oak driver who had taken over the 'Bulldog'.

The latter was in poor shape, but the pannier got them safely to Chippenham, and on to Swindon where a 'Hall' was waiting to take the train on to Paddington. The roar of the pannier's exhaust storming out to Box and then on down the gradient from Corsham to Chippenham was only matched by that of the '45XX' 2-6-2 tank in the previous chapter.

In later years the value of the '5700' class became appreciated in distant parts. As the introduction of diesel shunters proceeded, these incomparable tank engines became redundant and under British Railways' ownership a few of them were transferred to Folkestone for banking duties up the tremendous gradients of the harbour branch. With the Swindon setting of the Stepheson link motion, and its *puissance* at low speeds they were ideal for that job. Of another 'foreign' assignment I have particular memories. A number of these engines were sold to London Transport, and were sometimes to be seen working in and out of the big rolling stock works and depot at Acton. For some time I served on a joint technical committee concerned with design and manufacture of apparatus for the Victoria line, and we used to meet in an office beside the line at Acton Town station. A colleague on that committee was an ex-steam locomotive man whose early training had been at St Rollox, and as those pannier tanks puffed across to the works with stores train, 'nipping' smartly between the swarms of Underground electric trains, I frequently noticed that my colleague's eyes were also straying to the windows as those brown-painted 0-6-0s went skipping by!

There were three varieties of the lighter standard pannier tank, first introduced in 1931. These had a total weight in

TABLE 25

LIGHT PANNIER TANKS : VARIETIES

Serial numbers	Coupled wheel diameter ft in	Boiler pressure psi	Nom. T/E lb	Autogear
5400-5424	5–2	165	14,780	Fitted
6400-6439	4–7½	165	16,510	Fitted
7400-7429	4–7½	180	18,010	Not fitted

working order of 46.6 tons, and a maximum axle load of 15.6 tons, as compared with 49 tons for the '5700' class, with a maximum axle load of 17 tons.

These again were very sprightly little engines though naturally they did not have the 'punch' of the larger '5700' class. The principal dimensions of the latter, compared to the '6400' and the two older standard classes are set out in Table 26.

TABLE 26

STANDARD PANNIER TANKS

Class	'1901'	'2700'	'5700'	'6400'
Coupled wheel				
diameter ft in	4–1½	4–7½	4–7½	4–7½
Cylinders diameter (in)	16	17½	17½	16½
Stroke (in)	24	24	24	24
Boiler pressure psi	165	180	200	165
Heating surfaces sq ft				
Tubes	870.9	1040.6	1075.7	1004.2
Firebox	76.3	102	102.3	81.8
Grate Area sq ft	11.2	15.45	15.3	16.76
Total weight in working				
order tons	36.15	46	49	46.6

Another excellent small-engine design introduced in the Collett era was the '4800' class of 0–4–2 tank. This fulfilled the need for a locomotive still lighter than the '6400' class, that should have a high route availability, and be capable of working auto-trains. The '4800' was designed in the tradition of the neo-Dean practice, and resulted in an extraordinarily smart and 'nippy' little engine. The boiler was slightly larger than that of the '1901' class of pannier tank, with a tube heating surface of 869.8sq ft, firebox 83.2sq ft and a grate area of 12.8sq ft. The boiler pressure was 165lb per square inch and with coupled wheel diameter of 5ft 2in; the nominal tractive effort was 13,900lb. The maximum axle-load was only 13.9 tons and the total weight of the engine in working order 41.3 tons. These pretty little engines, of which a total of ninety-five was built, entirely preserved the 'rural' character of many a Great Western branch line. There were two groups of these engines. A total of seventy-five, fitted for autotrain working were originally numbered 4800-4874, while another twenty, Nos 5800 to 5819 were not fitted. The former series were later renumbered 1400 to 1474.

But appearances, and the sentimental attachment to the old-time atmosphere of Great Western branch lines, is only one aspect of the interesting impact the introduction of the '4800' class 0–4–2s had upon the Great Western motive power stud as a whole. There is nothing like a run on the footplate to dispel any thoughts of nostalgia or sentiment! I had an interesting experience of this when I rode No 1423 on the 11.55am auto-train from Fishguard Harbour to Clarbeston Road in 1947. One sometimes uses the term 'Rolls-Royce' to describe a motive power unit that is exceptionally quiet and smooth in going about its lawful occasions. Engine No 1423 was certainly one of these. She was a joy to ride, and through the fine countryside of West Pembrokeshire the run to Clarbeston Road was exhilarating. True we had only two coaches, but the ease with which that engine ran on a difficult road literally thrilled me. I was in the midst of making a series of footplate journeys on the larger Great Western engines, and boarded No 1423 more out of curiosity than anything else— but then just look at the way we ran from Wolf's Castle onwards! From the start, in $1\frac{3}{4}$ miles, half falling at 1 in 110 and half level, we attained 57mph; a bank of $1\frac{3}{4}$ miles rising at 1 in 110 was cleared at 48mph, and when the gradient eased to 1 in 163 speed rose rapidly to 55mph. So we ran the 6 miles from Wolf's Castle to Clarbeston Road in no more than 8min 27sec start to stop. This was a very smart timing seeing that the distance includes many more adverse than favourable gradients.

In 1910 five short-wheelbase 0–6–0 saddle tank engines with outside cylinders had been built for shunting in dock areas and other localities where sharp curves abound. They were handsome little things, with the saddle tank extending forward only as far as the front of the boiler barrel. In 1934 some further engines of this type were required, and in accordance with current practice they were built as pannier tanks. They had only 16in by 20in cylinders, coupled wheels 3ft 8in diameter, and had a boiler pressure of 165lb per square inch. The total weight in working order was $35\frac{3}{4}$ tons. The saddle tanks of 1910 were numbered 1361-5, and the new engines of 1934 were 1366 to 1371. Their total wheelbase was 11ft 0in against the 15ft 6in of the standard '5700' class.

CHAPTER 10

Outstanding Express Runs

THE standard of express passenger train running maintained
by a railway company can generally be considered as the most
definite end-product of its design and constructional practice.
There are exceptions, of course, such as those of railways
carrying a predominantly freight traffic. But in most developed countries it is the express passenger service that makes
the most severe demands upon the staying power of locomotives. As a corollary it is the most thermally efficient and reliable locomotives that permit an administration to operate the
most enterprising train services. However unbiased an observer wishes to be, and readers of my own work will know I
have some strong affections elsewhere, there can be no doubt
that the Great Western Railway was leading the country both
in locomotive performance and in speed of train service during the first few years of the grouping era. While standards
all over the country improved, the Great Western supremacy
was maintained until the early 1930s, when both the LMS and
the LNER began to advance to a far greater extent. Then it
was more a matter of managerial policy rather than through
any diminution in technical standards that the one-time pre-
eminence of Swindon was equalled and then surpassed. In a
number of earlier books dealing particularly with new types,
I have written extensively of locomotive running on the
Great Western, in such a way perhaps as to give something of
the overall picture. In this chapter I have brought together a
number of runs that involved performance beyond the general level of everyday excellence, because of varying exceptional circumstances.

In the summer of 1925 following the brilliant debut of the
'Castle' class locomotives, and their resounding success in the

Page 147. (above) The City of Truro *in York Railway Museum, 1933;* (below) The City of Truro, *as No 3440, in service in 1957, at Kingswear prior to the run described on page 109*

Page 148. (above) *5.0pm up express from Chester, near Wrexham: engine No* 2930 Saint Vincent, *with the author on the footplate;* (below) *'Bulldog' class* 4–4–0 No 3454 Skylark *on special excursion to Swindon, near Uffington*

Interchange Trials with the LNER, performance had moved into a veritably golden age on the GWR. By midsummer, however, there were still no more than twenty 'Castles' in service, mostly working from Old Oak Common, and in lengthy days of lineside observation both near Reading and in South Devon the number of 'Castles' spotted could be counted on the fingers of one hand. The Churchward 'Stars' were at the very zenith of their achievements, though I must admit still to looking back with not a little wonder at the two runs that I logged within a single fortnight in July of 1925. The first of the two was made on the 12.0 noon 'Torbay Limited' on the last Friday before the full summer service came into operation. The train then called at Exeter, and carried additionally a through portion for Penzance. In the following week, as usual then, it commenced running non-stop between Paddington and Torquay. So we had on that Friday a maximum load—thirteen 70ft coaches, nearly all of the latest smooth-sided stock, and weighing 469 tons tare. Instead of having the relief accorded to the Cornish Riviera Express of a load progressively reduced by slip portions, we had the full load of 500 tons gross behind the tender to be taken through to Exeter in the level three hours. Furthermore, although it was a Friday and consequently an Old Oak turn, no 'Castle' was available, and this vast load was worked by a 'Star', No 4042 *Prince Albert*. The day fortunately was perfect, and the engine in immaculate condition.

The actual start out of Paddington was extremely vigorous, passing Westbourne Park in 3min 5sec, but the driver had necessarily to conserve his resources faced with such a haulage proposition, and the engine was quickly linked up. The resulting acceleration was gradual, passing Ealing at 50mph, Southall at 55, West Drayton at 60, and reaching a maximum 65mph on the level at Slough. Already, however, the Churchward target of drawbar pull was being attained, though 2min had been dropped on the sharp initial timing of 37min to Reading. We were going well up the Kennet Valley regaining a little on our point-to-point schedule times, when a slack for relaying near Kintbury was succeeded by a most inopportune dead stand for signals in Hungerford station. We could not have been stopped at a much worse place, for not only had

149

J

this very heavy train to be restarted on a gradient of 1 in 114, followed by 1 in 220, but we had lost all chance of taking a run at the stiff final ascent to Savernake. When the signal cleared, however, and Driver Perry got his engine away without a suspicion of a slip in these difficult circumstances, I hardly believed that we should be at rest in St David's station Exeter, 112.2 miles away, in precisely two hours, having averaged 56mph over by far the most difficult part of the route.

We were not able to attain more than 48mph before tackling the stiff final 3 miles up to Savernake; but we were still doing 41½mph on passing Wolfhall Junction, and on the last ¾-mile, on 1 in 145-106, we did not go below 41mph. Here the engine was developing about 1,400 drawbar horsepower, to which the tremendous percussion of the exhaust bore vivid audible witness! But the Kintbury and Hungerford checks had between them cost 7½min in running, and we were now 9¾min late. Some fine speed was put on down to Westbury, with a maximum of 80½mph at Lavington, and then, of course, we had the handicap of travelling through both Westbury and Frome stations, with severe speed restrictions at both, and the disadvantage of tackling the sharp climbs, first to Milepost 114¼ and then to 122¾, from relatively low initial speeds. The Westbury and Frome by-pass lines were then very much things of the future. Although now carrying a distinctly abnormal load we kept the hard point-to-point time of 22½min for the 19.7 miles from Westbury to Castle Cary. Maximum speed was 75mph down the Bruton bank, and we were going splendidly at 72mph beyond Castle Cary when we were slowed once again for permanent way repairs before Keinton Mandeville: another 2½min lost!

Although with a fine recovery and a top speed of 73mph near Langport we had won back to no more than 8min late on passing Cogload Junction, 137.9 miles from Paddington in 151min 55sec, the tremendous climb up to Whiteball Tunnel lay ahead—tremendous that is for a 'Star' class engine hauling a load of 500 tons. Splendidly though we had done from Hungerford, covering the 76.4 miles from that intermediate stop in 81min 50sec, despite the check at Keinton Mandeville, the driver would have been fully justified on the basis of load alone in stopping for assistance up to Whiteball. In bad rail conditions, with the risk of stalling on the 1 in 80 gradient he would probably have stopped for rear-end banking help from Wellington. But the running conditions were ideal, and this huge load was taken up the gradient single-handed. Taunton was passed at 56mph. Up the gradually steepening road to Wellington, with gradients increasing from 1 in 369 to 1 in 170, speed fell to 47½mph and thus we attacked the bank itself: 3 miles at 1 in 90-86-90 to the tunnel entrance and then ¾-mile at 1 in 127 through the tunnel itself. The performance here was magnificent. The speed on entering the tunnel was still as high as 30mph, but it fell further to 25½mph before the summit was passed. The 10.9 miles of ascent from Taunton had taken 14min 55sec which was considerably faster than could have been achieved if a stop had been made at Wellington for a banker. After that we ran fast down to Exeter, making an average speed of 75mph over the 11.4 miles from Tiverton Junction to Stoke Canon. So we stopped in Exeter St Davids, 173.7 miles from Paddington, in 190min 10sec. We were 10¼min late in it is true; but the delays experienced en route accounted for all that, and our net time was exactly the 180min booked. Seeing that when the Cornish Riviera Express left Paddington with loads of this magnitude, such loads were reduced by the detaching of slip portions to about 430 tons from Westbury, and 360 from Taunton, our driver had done a grand job in running to the same schedule with a load of 500 tons throughout.

A fortnight later I was a passenger on the 5.8pm up from Newton Abbot, just a week before the August Bank Holiday week-end, when exceptional traffic, causing extreme dislocation on the Torquay line, led to a very late start. Combined with the Cornish part of the train the load was again thirteen coaches, though of somewhat lighter stock, of 421 tons tare; but the train was subjected to various delays, and a further 15min had been lost by the time we reached Taunton. Here, three more coaches were added—through coaches from Ilfracombe and Minehead, and a slip coach which this train then detached at Newbury. With this addition we had the truly colossal load, for that time, of 514 tons tare, and packed with passengers returning from holidays, fully 550 tons gross behind the tender. Once again the engine was an unassisted 'Star', No 4026 then named *King Richard,* and driven by Walter Springthorpe of Old Oak Common shed. With the train so much out of its normal path delays were perhaps to be expected, and we were stopped for ½-min shortly after leaving Taunton, at a point 142¼ miles from Paddington. But after that we got an absolutely clear road right to Westbourne Park, and passed Old Oak Common West Box, 138.9 miles from the second start at Taunton, in the remarkable time of 147min 5sec—a start to pass average speed of 56.8mph. A load of 'fifteen' was still being conveyed even after the detaching of the slip coach at Newbury, from when the load was 515 tons behind the tender.

Because of the initial check we lost 5min between Taunton and Cogload Junction; but the point-to-point timing of 134min for the 127.8 miles onwards to Southall was kept with ½-min to spare—a running average of 57.3mph. This involved some very hard work intermediately. The Bruton bank, from Castle Cary, is almost as severe as Whiteball and up this our 550-ton train was taken at a minimum speed of 24mph. We slackened speed carefully through Frome and Westbury stations, and then the crew got some wonderful work out of the engine on the long ascent to Savernake. Up this gradient speed averaged 54mph for 25.5 miles, and on the hardest stretch—6 miles at 1 in 222 from Lavington— the speed fell to a sustained 48mph. Here the engine was developing about 1,350 drawbar horsepower, and exerting a drawbar pull of 4.7 tons. This was 38 per cent of the nominal tractive effort of the locomotive and an outstanding effort in the middle of a long-sustained hard run. Savernake summit was cleared at 53mph after which we ran fast down to Reading, averaging 72mph from Bedwyn to Theale, 25.2 miles. We had dropped 1¼min on our point-to-point allowance of 106min for the 101.9 miles from Cogload Junction to Reading, but with the slightly reduced load of 515 tons a magnificent concluding effort was made. Speed rose on dead level track, to 69mph at Slough, and the average over the 19.9 miles from Maidenhead to Acton was 66mph. The drawbar horsepower here was 965, with a drawbar pull of about 2½ tons. So despite the initial signal stop the 139.6 miles from Taunton to Old Oak Common West Box we covered in 150 min. Signal checks in conclusion caused the last 3.3 miles into Paddington to take 8min; but the net time for the 142.9 miles was not a second outside the 152min scheduled.

In contrast to these Herculean feats of haulage, by locomotives of 1910 vintage, the working of the high-speed Cheltenham Flyer was sometimes dismissed, even among ardent Great Western supporters, as a very easy job. Certainly physical and traffic conditions, quite apart from any questions of locomotive capacity, favoured the making of a spectacular start to stop average speed from Swindon to Paddington: $77\frac{1}{4}$ miles of almost perfect road, with negligible curvature, slightly falling gradients for part of the way, and at 3.45pm a line relatively free of conflicting traffic. Yet to belittle the achievement, by which the start-to-stop timing of the 2.30pm express from Cheltenham was reduced from 75min first to 70, then to 67 and finally to 65min—the last giving an average speed of 71.3mph—would be to miss something of the significance of Great Western locomotive performance in the grouping era. Even when the effort was stepped up, under specially organised conditions, to make a world record in June 1932, with an average speed of 81.7mph from start to stop, the locomotive concerned, No 5006 *Tregenna Castle*, was at no point pressed beyond a nominal optimum condition of steaming. Furthermore, that the achievement of June 1932 did not represent the ultimate in high speed running performance of the 'Castle' class locomotives, was shown five years later when slightly faster times were made over the major part of the route with a train heavier by one coach.

In Table 27 the summary details of the above two runs are set out, and also one run on which I was a passenger, and which is interesting because it was made in very bad weather conditions.

The first is the 'world record' run of 5 June 1932 while the second is the still more remarkable run of 30 June, 1937 when the times of the 'world record' had been surpassed, until the engine *Rhuddlan Castle* was drastically eased down after Southall. The third run was made on a raw winter's night against an easterly wind with driving sleet and rain, and the driver was doing his best to recover something of a ten-minute late start from Swindon.

TABLE 27

THE 'CHELTENHAM FLYER'

Run No	1	2	3
Engine No	5006	5039	5025
Engine Name	*Tregenna Castle*	*Rhuddlan Castle*	*Chirk Castle*
Load tons gross	195	235	270
Distance	Actual	Actual	Actual
Miles	m s	m s	m s
0.0 SWINDON	0 00	0 00	0 00
5.7 Shrivenham	6 15	6 35	7 02
24.2 Didcot	18 55	18 57	20 44
41.3 Reading	30 11	30 27	33 17
58.8 Slough	42 10	42 08	45 50
68.2 Southall	48 51	48 46	52 43
77.3 PADDINGTON	56 47	61 07	62 15
Average speed: Shrivenham- Southall mph	88.0	88.6	82.1
Max. speed mph	92	95	$86\frac{1}{2}$

It is now important to look at details of the engine working. On the 'world record' run *Tregenna Castle* was being
driven with the regulator full open from Shrivenham onwards and cut-off mostly in 17 per cent. It is always difficult
and sometimes very misleading to make judgment of the technical aspects of locomotive performance by figures of cut-off
and regulator openings, because of the inevitable variations
between one engine and another. But from much footplate
experience of the 'Castle' class locomotives I have found that
they display very similar characteristics, and that 17 or 18
per cent is the normal cut-off for fast express running. Some
drivers preferred to run with a regulator opening a little less
than full for hard work. With medium-degree superheating,
as standard on all Great Western 4–6–0 locomotives in the
Churchward–Collett era, a slight closing of the regulator provided the wire-drawing necessary to give a little extra superheat, and some drivers considered that the engines ran more
freely in these conditions, possibly due to the additional

superheat in the steam. On the bad night when I travelled behind *Chirk Castle* on the Cheltenham Flyer the driver worked this way, but in combating the east wind and the heavier load he found it necessary to use 20 per cent cut off throughout from Shrivenham. But the main point of this particular discussion is to emphasise that *Tregenna Castle* was not worked inordinately hard to make the world record —far from it. Neither was *Rhuddlan Castle,* making the even faster times, and a maximum of 95mph near Didcot.

Reverting to the 'Stars', I have mentioned earlier the very fine traditions of running maintained by the top link crews at Wolverhampton. This was displayed better perhaps than anywhere else in the working of the very important 6.10pm express down from Paddington. This was one of the two-hour Birmingham trains, normally detaching slip coaches at Bicester and Banbury, and making one intermediate stop at Leamington. The successive reductions in load relieved the burden of engine and crew as the journey progressed, and enabled the fast time of 26min start-to-stop to be booked over the 23.3 miles from Leamington to Birmingham, despite the markedly adverse gradients on this section. But on one recorded occasion in 1925, for some reason that was unexplained at the time, no slip coaches were available—and while the passengers for Bicester and Banbury were accommodated in separate coaches stops had to be made at both stations to detach these coaches. Furthermore there was at that time an engineering slack of extreme severity near Greenford, when the Great West Road was under construction. Consequently a full 5min was lost at the very start, and speed had not risen to more than 61½mph when the ascent of the Gerrards Cross bank was commenced. The load from Paddington was one of 340 tons tare, 365 tons full and the engine No 4067 *Tintern Abbey.* A minute had been regained on passing High Wycombe, and then there commenced a truly outstanding effort.

Up the 1 in 164 gradient from West Wycombe to Saunderton speed rose to 55mph, involving an output of 1,350 drawbar horsepower, and a drawbar pull of roughly 4 tons! This was equal to 33 per cent of the nominal tractive effort of the locomotive. A tremendous acceleration followed, to a maximum speed of exactly 90mph at Haddenham, and despite the initial check the train reached Bicester, 53.4 miles, in 61¼min. The net time of 56¼min was nearly 2min less than the time normally booked to pass, at full speed. Not a great deal could be done onwards to Banbury, with a steeply uphill start, and the necessity to reduce speed over Aynho Junction. Consequently this 14.1 miles took 17¼min instead of the usual 14min pass to pass. But a most brilliant spurt followed to Leamington. With speeds of 85mph near Fenny Compton, and no less than 92mph in the descent of Fosse Road bank, the 19.8 miles from Banbury to Leamington took only 19min 40sec. The initial delay, plus the cost of making the two additional stops, amounted to a total of 15min in running, and left a net time of 83¼min against the normal non-stop scheduled time of 91min. The load had been reduced to 335 tons from Bicester, and to 305 tons from Banbury. To gain nearly 8min net on schedule with this sharply booked train certainly placed this run in the gallery of outstanding achievements. J. Williams of Wolverhampton was the driver.

It is next the turn of the 'Saint' class. For some little time after the Bristolian express was put on in 1935, it was worked regularly by a 'King' class locomotive. The departure time from Paddington was then 10am and the engine remained at Bristol during the afternoon to work the return train at 4.30pm. It was not a difficult turn, and the standard of punctuality in both directions was high. Several expert recorders made journeys by the train in the hopes of securing something exceptional in the way of performance, but nothing transpired until one day in the summer of 1936, when the late R. E. Charlewood was a passenger. There was the usual seven-coach train, with a gross load of 225 tons behind the tender. From Paddington with engine No 6015 *King Richard III* the running was at first unusually good; but then the engine 'ran hot', and a stop had to be made at Reading to secure a substitute. A 'Saint' No 2937 *Clevedon Court* was obtained almost at a moment's notice, and after a stop of just under 7min the train started again, leaving Reading 12min after the train was normally due to pass through, at high speed. The London driver and his fireman had transferred to No 2937 and at once they set out to make exceptional times. It was a pity that the operating was not everywhere up to the same standard of keenness as the locomotive work, for three moderate signal checks were experienced that had every sign of being due to dilatoriness in pulling off the distants! One would imagine that news had passed down the line that the engine of the Bristolian had failed, and the signalmen were not expecting her to come up as rapidly as she actually did.

All that apart, however, Driver Jones and his mate got some wonderful work out of *Clevedon Court*. From the Reading start they passed Didcot (milepost 53¼), 17¼ miles, in 15min 53sec after having sustained 76 to 78mph, and then followed a couple of infuriating checks to 60mph at Steventon, and 55mph at Wantage Road. Then came some magnificent speed. On the gradually rising length to Swindon, where the Cheltenham Flyer made its records in the *opposite* direction, speed was worked up to 83½mph near Shrivenham. There was a slight easing through Swindon to 78mph and then followed a full 90mph at the foot of Dauntsey bank—only the second known instance of such a maximum with the 'Saint' class engines. Then having made an average of 80.7mph between mileposts 64 and 92 the train was checked to 46½mph at Chippenham, through what was probably another lazy 'pull-off'. After a most vigorous recovery, up 1 in 660, to 72½mph at Corsham, no exceptional speed was attempted downhill through Box Tunnel, and the approach to Bath was at moderate speed. But despite those three annoying signal checks the 70.9 miles from Reading to Bath had taken no more than 59½min or only a minute more than the pass-to-pass schedule time of the Bristolian. A fast recovery to 76½mph on the level at Keynsham brought the train into Bristol in 72½min from Reading, despite two more slight checks.

On arrival at Temple Meads the train had still averaged more than 60mph from Paddington, despite the stop to change engines at Reading, and the five slight checks on the second stage of the run. The total time for the 118.3 miles was 117 min 17sec, and the running time 110min 20sec. But included in this was the spell when *King Richard III* was limping along with a hot bearing, and *Clevedon Court's* net time of 69min over the 82.3 miles from Reading to Bristol showed an average speed of 71.6mph.

Another journey when unusually severe running conditions prevailed was a trip of my own on the 6.10pm express from Paddington to Wolverhampton. This was a counterpart, on the north road, to my journey on the Torbay Limited in that a very heavy initial load was taken through to destination without any of the usual reductions through the detaching of slip portions. The day was the Friday before Whitsun 1930. Several 'King' class locomotives were stationed at Wolverhampton by that time, but it so happened that for a few weeks prior to the holiday one of these engines did not seem to be available for the 6.10pm. That hardest of all the Birmingham two-hour trains was being worked day after day, week after week, by engine No 4088 *Dartmouth Castle*. It was at that time I was living in Ealing, and passing through Paddington on my way home from Kings Cross I saw the 6.10pm express nearly every day. On the Friday, when I was travelling to Barrow-in-Furness, via Chester (!), the train was divided. The various slip coaches were carried on the second portion, and the first part of the train took the enormous load, for this schedule, of 440 tons tare, 475 tons full, right through to Wolverhampton, and as usual *Dartmouth Castle* was the engine. Again the occasion was favoured with good weather, and a supremely competent driver in A. Taylor, of Stafford Road shed. Apart from two slight signal checks before we had cleared the main line at Old Oak Common we had a clear road for the entire journey to Wolverhampton.

By dint of some very hard driving, and some equally skilful firing, the sectional point-to-point times of this express were maintained with remarkable accuracy, and passing Banbury dead on time in 71min 55sec for the 67.5 miles from Paddington the job was virtually 'in the bag', so far as timekeeping to Leamington was concerned. Justifiably, in the circumstances, some of the speed restrictions were interpreted rather liberally, such as 50mph (instead of 35) through High Wycombe, and an unchecked 69mph over Aynho Junction. But the carriage in which I was riding rode quite smoothly at all points. With such a huge load the uphill speeds were a little on the slow side, such as 51mph up the 1 in 254 to Beaconsfield, $41\frac{1}{2}$mph up the 1 in 167 to Saunderton, and a minimum of $52\frac{1}{2}$mph up the 1 in 200 to Ardley. There was some fast running downhill, with 83½mph descending from Princes Risborough to Haddenham, and a long sustained 74 to 78mph from Fenny Compton to the point of slowing down for the stop at Leamington. Our times at the booked timing points were as follows:

TABLE 28

Distance Miles		Sch min	Actual min sec	
0.0	PADDINGTON	0	0	00
—			sigs.	
3.3	*Old Oak Common West*	7	7	20
7.8	Greenford	13	12	55
10.3	Northolt Junction	15½	15	35
26.5	High Wycombe	32	32	15
34.7	Princes Risborough	41	42	30
44.1	*Ashendon Junction*	49	49	40
53.4	Bicester	58	58	15
62.4	*Aynho Junction*	67	67	15
67.5	Banbury	72	71	55
87.3	LEAMINGTON	91	89	50

Seeing that the schedule was originally planned for an initial load of about 400 tons from Paddington, reduced by one coach at both Bicester and Banbury, the above was truly remarkable going for a 'Castle' with an unchanged load of 475 tons.

Normally the train stopped for 3min at Leamington, but on this occasion we stopped for 6¼min on account of holiday traffic, and although we had arrived one minute early we left 2min late. It wase almost inevitable that further time would be lost onwards to Birmingham, for the schedule of 26min was planned for a load of little more than 300 tons. The great obstacle is of course Hatton Bank with its 3 miles of 1 in 110. There are a little under 3 miles of broken gradient in which to take a run at it, and there speed was worked up to 45mph. Then on the bank itself speed fell to 32¼mph, and Hatton station, 6.2 miles, was passed in 10¼min. The gradients continue adverse, though not so severely, to Solihull before a very gradual descent towards Birmingham commences. Very fine work was involved in running the 13.9 miles from Hatton to Tyseley in 14¾min. There was a slight slowing for permanent way work at Bordesley, and Birmingham Snow Hill was reached in 29½min from Leamington. The total time from Paddington was 2hr 5½min; but as we had spent 3min station overtime at Leamington, and another minute could be debited to the Old Oak and Bordesley checks, only 1½min of that 5½min late arrival in Birmingham could be chalked up against the engine and her crew. That deficit, incredibly small in the circumstances, was immediately wiped out, for the concluding 12.6 miles on to Wolverhampton—a very hard stretch with no opportunity for fast running—were covered in 18¼min instead of the 20min allowed. The total running time for the 110.6 miles from Paddington to Birmingham was 119min 20sec and for the 123.2 miles to Wolverhampton, 137 min 35sec representing average speeds of 55.7 and 53.7mph respectively: wonderful work for a 'Castle' hauling a gross trailing load of 475 tons.

In Chapter 6 I referred to some outstanding hill climbing efforts of 'King' class locomotives on this same train. For some years prior to the outbreak of World War I the late George P. Antrobus was an almost daily traveller between Paddington and Leamington, and his voluminous records include some remarkable feats of performance. At one time the earlier stages of the journey were chronically delayed, week after week, by engineering slacks on account of the widening works preparatory to the laying in of the 'tube' line to Ruislip, and on one such day the train was so checked as to pass High Wycombe 8min late. Even so, this did not represent the full extent of the initial delays because 2min had already been regained. The engine was the *King Edward IV*, No 6017, with a gross trailing load of 445 tons. Once clear of the affected area the driver set out to regain the lost time with a vengeance, and to appreciate fully the extent to which he opened the engine out I must refer to the full dress trials conducted on engine No 6001 in 1952 on the Swindon stationary plant. The limit of steaming, with *two* firemen taking turns at the shovelling was a little over 30,000lb per hour and the maximum that could be expected continuously from a single fireman was 25,000lb per hour. At the higher rate, with two firemen the power output at 55mph was 1,430 at the drawbar.

On this ordinary service journey on the 6.10pm train, once High Wycombe was passed the engine was pounded well and truly, accelerating up the 1 in 167 gradient to Saunderton until 54½mph was attained. This involved an output of 1,785 equivalent drawbar horsepower or 350hp more than Swindon secured with *two* firemen at the same speed! Far from being short of steam after this effort *King Edward IV* put on some terrific speed downhill, reaching 91½mph at Haddenham; and by continuing in the same style the lateness was reduced to 6½min at Ashendon Junction, 5min at Aynho Junction, 4¾min at Banbury, and by some further very fast running in conclusion the arrival in Leamington was only 2min late. At the same time the train was carrying its normal loading and this was reduced by the detaching of successive slip coaches, to 405 tons at Bicester and 335 tons at Banbury. From the load point of view this 'King' class engine had an easier task than *Dartmouth Castle*. On the run with *King Edward IV* the principal times were:

TABLE 29

Distance Miles		Sch min	Actual min sec	
0.0	PADDINGTON	0	0	00
10.3	Northolt Junction	15½	checks	
26.5	High Wycombe	32	40	04
34.7	Princes Risborough	42	49	10
44.1	*Ashendon Junction*	49½	55	57
53.4	Bicester	58½	63	59
62.4	*Aynho Junction*	67	72	00
67.5	Banbury	72	76	44
87.3	LEAMINGTON	90½	92	59

The intermediate point-to-point times had been modified since my journey in 1930, and the working time of arrival in Leamington was 90½min. But the net time on this truly splendid journey was 83min, a gain of 7½min on the working schedule. The driver was Glover, of Stafford Road shed.

CHAPTER 11

Locomotives of Precision

IN 1955 a distinguished son of Swindon, Kenneth J. Cook, took office as president of the Institution of Locomotive Engineers. At that time he was far away at Doncaster, sitting in the chair once occupied by Sir Nigel Gresley; but as at an earlier date he had also sat in the chair of Churchward at Swindon, it was, as he said, not surprising that there had been some cross-breeding. When he described in his presidential address some of the workshop practice he had applied to the locomotives of the former LNER it was evident that his earlier experience was deeply ingrained and his devotion to the Great Western as fervent as ever. He admitted that it was his original intention to entitle his address: 'The British Locomotive, a Machine of Beauty and Precision'. He then went on to explain that he considered 'Until 1950 that would not have been inapt, but with the advent of certain engines with a strong continental or transatlantic appearance, it was thought that this would not now be suitable.' Having taken this subtle 'swipe' at the appearance of the British Standard Locomotives he eventually chose as his title: 'The Steam Locomotive, a Machine of Precision'. Although not mentioned as such all his hearers knew well that the earlier experience he described was entirely Great Western, and it was the development of Great Western practice in the years after nationalisation that he applied so successfully at Doncaster and Darlington.

In view of the 'fancy' designs and methods developed at Swindon—to quote the adjective used to me by one of Sir Nigel Gresley's successors—it is interesting at the outset to recall some of the items of expense involve in the maintenance and running of Great Western locomotives as compared with those of the other railways in the grouping era. The year 1937

affords a good time for such a comparison, because then the
LMS was climbing well out of the trials and tribulations of
the amalgamation, and on the LNER the reign of Sir Nigel
Gresley was reaching the zenith of its achievement. I have
not, in fairness, included the figures of the Southern, because
at that time the steam locomotive had become the very Cin-
derella of the motive power organisation.

TABLE 30

LOCOMOTIVE MAINTENANCE AND RUNNING COSTS
1937

	GWR	LMS	LNER
Repairs and Partial Renewals			
Per engine	£401	£434	£476
Per engine mile	3.51d	3.50d	4.35d
Running expenses excluding fuel			
Per train mile	18.95d	20.39d	20.74d
Per engine	£1476	£1714	£1569
Wages, connecting with locomotive running			
Per train mile	11.72d	11.67d	12.2d
Per engine	£913	£981	£917
Coal			
Per train mile	6.34d	7.55d	7.44d
Per engine	£494	£635	£563
Water			
Per train mile	0.33d	0.51d	0.56d
Per engine	£26	£43	£42
Lubricants			
Per train mile	0.14d	0.16d	0.14d
Per engine	£10	£14	£11
Stock of engines	3,632	7,657	6,576

From these official statistics, compiled from the published reports of the companies, it will be seen that except in respect
of the repair and partial renewal costs, when related to the
engine miles run, the Great Western showed notably lower
figures than its northern neighbours. In other words the degree of standardisation, in design and fittings, and the pre-

cision methods used in the three main workshops at Swindon, Wolverhampton and Caerphilly were paying off handsomely.

I turn now more particularly to the precision methods used for locomotive construction and repair in Great Western workshops. Mr Cook considered that in the decade that was ending in 1939 the British steam locomotive was still in the ascendant, and well able to hold its own against other forms of prime mover, both on economic as well as on mechanical grounds. There were then plentiful supplies of large coal, shed maintenance was at its best, and the continuity of railway employment was attractive. Quite apart from that, I am sure it can be said that the great majority of men on the payroll of the locomotive department had 'steam in the blood' and would not willingly have changed their jobs for any other. At the same time, quite apart from its vaguely-defined yet strong emotional appeal, the steam locomotive is a most fascinating machine from a scientific point of view. To quote Kenneth Cook:

> The basic mechanism of an orthodox locomotive is unique in that its power is transmitted equally through two, three or more axes whose centres are partly fixed but are subject to considerable movement relative to their locations and to each other. Concentrated power is transmitted between the axes by rigid couplings subject to rotating and alternating tensional and compressive forces. These movements, caused from within the locomotive by its direct and induced forces, and from without by irregularities of the track, have an effect upon the dimensions between axis centres, and argument may therefore develop as to whether extreme basic accuracy is necessary. It is true that if there are errors in original setting, the movement of axles during motion and power transmission may tend to cancel them out; but they may equally add to the error and also to the stresses set up. It is therefore fairly clear that the greater the original accuracy the lower will be the maximum stresses set up in the components, and it also enables initial tolerances of working parts to be reduced to a minimum. This in itself reduces hammering effects in bearings, and the rate at which wear and slackness develop.

The degree of robustness with which the steam locomotive had to be built in order to withstand and accommodate itself to irregularities in the track was not always appreciated outside the experienced locomotive drawing offices and works. I remember vividly the surprise expressed by certain manu-

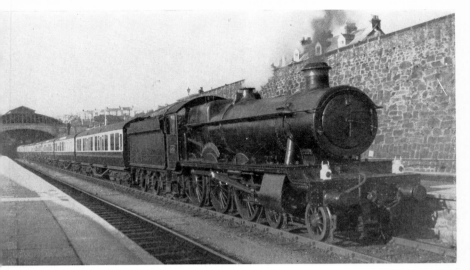

Page 165. (above) *Up Cornish Riviera Express, ready to start from Penzance, engine No 5915* Trentham Hall; *(below) engine No 4920* Dumbleton Hall *going hard with the 8.30am Plymouth to Paddington having replaced a disabled visiting engine during the Interchange Trials of 1948*

Page 166. (above) *One of the Moguls in plain green standard* GWR *livery, No 4375;* (centre) *2–8–2 heavy freight tank engine No 7210 in* BR *livery;* (below) *a Mogul, No 6385, fully lined out in green, in* BR *days*

facturers of road transport equipment, which was at first applied without alteration to diesel multiple unit sets, when that equipment rattled itself to pieces in record time in railway service. They learned the difference between road conditions and the running of steel tyres on steel rails in very much the hard way. And if the relatively light loading conditions of a multiple-unit railcar could wreak such havoc, how infinitely more severe were the conditions on the more modern steam locomotives. How could any degree of precision be built into their construction? Yet Churchward himself laid the foundations of improved constructional practice, by establishing such accuracy in the setting out of frames with solid instead of adjustable big-ends; and Collett, as a workshop specialist, developed a number of practices that were of great interest and value.

During the most fruitful period of this development Collett was well served in the works at Swindon by two men of outstanding 'shop' ability: the locomotive works manager, R. A. G. Hannington and his assistant, Kenneth J. Cook. Both were, to a greater degree perhaps than Collett himself, men of a railway outlook extending far beyond purely manufacturing methods. With the 'King' class locomotives, after repairs at Swindon, Hannington used to take each one for its trial trip personally. It was no perfunctory running in business. They used to go to Didcot, wait until the down line was clear to the outskirts of Swindon, and assured of 'line clear' for some twenty miles, hey presto, each engine was driven up to a sustained 100mph! Whether the civil engineer knew anything of these exploits is another matter, but the fact remains that unless Hannington was satisfied with the behaviour of the engines under these conditions they were not passed for return to ordinary traffic.

The most important advance in locomotive erection and repair methods introduced during the Collett–Hannington–Cook period was the use of optical methods of ensuring accuracy in the setting of axles in relation to each other and to the cylinder centre-lines. Cook emphasised how there are two ingredients contributing to accuracy in locomotive mechanisms that are not always appreciated in their several ways. The first is accuracy of measurement, and the second is the degree

167

K

of accuracy that one can work to the measurements specified. In a steam locomotive 'measurement' had to cater for three-dimensional requirements over a wide area, and upwards of a hundred years of experience—at Swindon at any rate—lay behind the practices that were then in vogue. In his presidential address to the Institution of Locomotive Engineers in 1955, Cook described the methods that had hitherto been established as standard.

> In the first place there are the cylinder centre lines throughout the length of the engine, with the axle centres to be located at right angles, and at correct distance from the cylinder barrels. For many years methods remained fairly uniform using simple apparatus in the form of fine cord or wire stretched from front cylinder faces to rear of engine, set by calipers from front and back of cylinders, meeting a 'straight edge' clamped on supports in the centre of the driving axle-box guides. The supports incorporated fixed or movable centres from which checks fore and aft to similar centres in adjacent axle-box guides could be made by trammels, either solid or adjustable. Check for normality of axis to cylinder centre line was by large steel squares, and for parallel of framing and guide edges to centre line by steel rule. Should right angle of axis not be proved, the lines had to be removed, adjustments to surfaces made and the lines and 'straight-edge' reset for checking.

Many hundreds of famous locomotives, not only on the Great Western but elsewhere, were erected by these simple yet rather primitive methods, and Cook comments pointedly: 'There was a good amount of subterfuge in the olden days for making lines appear to run true, and in the subsequent machining of components it was generally assumed that wear or inaccuracies were equal on either side of the engine. Nevertheless with good craftsmen working under favourable conditions fairly good results were obtained, and high speed locomotives were repaired and maintained on these methods, although in general at the expense of slack initial fits of some wearing parts.' The emphasis on good craftsmanship was particularly evident in the celebrated 'A' shop at Swindon. Yet even so, even with the highest standards of craftsmanship there would be bound to be variations in the standards of erection. Prior to Churchward's day I think it can be said that the practice of Crewe works was unsurpassed in England. Yet even with all the devices introduced by the redoubtable F. W. Webb they managed to turn out one of his celebrated three-cylinder compounds that was not 'square'! And a fine packet of trouble she was in traffic! !

In the late 1920s the well-known German optical instrument firm of Zeiss produced a telescope working in conjunction with an auxiliary telescope used to detect errors in alignment. This subsidiary device is known as a collimator. Instead of using a stretched wire or cord to reproduce 'in the solid' the extension of the cylinder centre line as shown on a drawing, the cylinder 'centre-line' took the form of the line of sight of a telescope, previously located in the cylinder itself. The collimator was mounted in the line of sight at right-angles to each set of horn guides in turn, and the detecting cross lines on the infinite scale of the collimator registered zero from the main telescope only if the collimator was correctly located in the line of sight. At the same time the collimator itself required to be accurately mounted distance-wise from the front face of the cylinder to fulfil the designed dimension of the locomotive. Having got the collimator located on the correct centre line and at the correct distance, subsidiary measuring instruments attached to the collimator and its mountings enabled the guide faces for the axle boxes to be established, and precision machinery to be set up for grinding the faces concerned to within fine limits. This apparatus was used for the erection of new locomotives, but perhaps to an even more important degree in the repair of existing ones.

When a locomotive came in for a 'heavy general' overhaul the entire frame and axle-box guides was surveyed by this optical method; and when all the necessary measurements had been taken it would be decided exactly what amount had to be taken off or added to each axle-box guide face. There could be a certain amount of give and take in the length from cylinder face to driving box guides, provided the cylinder clearance was maintained. By using this degree of tolerance, one way or the other the amount of metal to be removed could be kept to a minimum to bring the axle-centres correct. These adjustments to the horn guides were specified to thousandths of an inch, indicating the degree of precision to which locomotives came to be built and repaired at Swindon. A newly-repaired 'Star' 'Castle' or 'King' became the nearest thing to a railway Rolls-Royce that I have ever encountered. As Cook emphasised in his presidential address the methods introduced at Swindon enabled the initial clearances provided in the working parts to be much less than was then normal in general locomotive practice. Or as another Swindon man expressed it graphically to me: 'We scrap at the clearances the others start with.'

In this connection I shall always remember an incident during the celebrated Interchange Trials between the Great Western and the LNER in 1925, as told to me by E. D. Trask the Doncaster engineer in charge of the Gresley Pacific No 4474 during her running between Paddington and Plymouth. There is no doubt that the Great Western men entered into this contest in a spirit of colossal superiority complex, particularly when they saw the size and *length* of their rival. As will be recalled, before the trials proper, on the Cornish Riviera Express, there was some preliminary running and on her first trip to Plymouth No 4474 went down on the heavy, but easily timed 1.30pm from Paddington to enable the visiting driver and fireman to take the measure of the road, and get used to the huge lumps of Welsh coal—which was so different from what they normally had on the LNER. There is no doubt that the curves worried the East Coast men, particularly those beyond Exeter. Then, when they reached Plymouth on the first trip and got down to Laira shed, the foreman fitter came up to the engine with his face wreathed in smiles, saying: 'I've won my bet all right!' Trask asked what he meant, and got the reply: 'I bet that if you ever got here, you'd never get back.' Again Trask was nonplussed, and the Plymouth man with ill-concealed pleasure pointed to the left-hand outside driving box, and the frame below, which was plastered with white metal, and certainly suggested a failure. The engine was moved over a pit and Trask made a thorough examination, to find all was well, and quite cool. What had happened was that on one of the sharp curves the clearance between coupling rod and axle box face had been tight, and a 'shaving' had been taken off, with no harmful effects. Trask surprised the somewhat crestfallen Laira man by saying: 'Fine; now we've got the clearance we want for this road of yours.' Certainly No 4474 ran the whole fortnight without the slightest mechanical trouble.

Nevertheless, the incident emphasised the essential difference that then existed between the shop practice of Doncaster and Swindon. All lineside observers were familiar with the 'Gresley ring', and the rhythmical clank of his motion, despite the lightness of the individual components. There was ample evidence of generous clearances in the bearings. Although it is not strictly part of the Great Western story a further experience of my own provides evidence of the success of the cross-breeding that Cook himself introduced between Swindon and Doncaster practice. When optical methods were applied to the repair of the Gresley 'Pacifics' a most astonishing change came over the manner of their running—not in power output, but in the sweetness and silence of their action. I rode an 'A3', not long out of Doncaster, over the very difficult and sharply-curved Waverley route from Carlisle to Edinburgh; and instead of the old familiar 'ring' and clanking she was just like a 'ghost' engine, and immensely strong on the banks.

In association with the increased accuracy of frame alignment was the workmanship put into the rods and the big ends. Cook explained in his presidential address that the term 'frame alignment' rather camouflaged the main quest. What was vitally important to a sweet running engine, and the maintenance of minimum clearances, was the setting up of the axle-centres relative to each other, together with the precise maintenance of the designed length of coupling rods, and of the throw and angle of the crank pins. But with these features as the major objective the complete alignment of the wheels relative to the framing was a natural corollary. Churchward to a large extent had set the parameters as long previously as the design of his standard two-cylinder 4–6–0 locomotives and the other outside cylindered engines in the first standard range. By insisting on a high degree of accuracy in erection he was able to adopt a solid big-end instead of the generally used adjustable type with cottered fastenings. These solid big-ends were standard on all Great Western outside cylindered locomotives; and by the use of optical methods of measurement and lining up the practice was facilitated, and still closer fits in the bearings made possible. For the inside big-ends of the four-cylinder engines a slight adaptation of the French de Glehn cottered type was standardised, and in the course of Cook's cross-breeding policy the Swindon–de Glehn big-end was substituted for the Doncaster marine type on the Gresley 'Pacifics'—with beneficial results.

While the introduction of the optical method of frame alignment, and all that went with it, was a major feather in the Swindon cap, the general standard of workmanship put into Great Western locomotives was very high—not only in large items such as boilers and fire-boxes, but also in the numerous fittings. Like Crewe in LNWR days the majority of the boiler fittings were 'home made', as a senior British Railways executive once remarked after nationalisation, and they were very beautifully made. In the course of my footplate work I have had occasion to see locomotives fitted with numerous gadgets of proprietary manufacture, and home-made ones too, particularly in the years immediately after World War II some of these gadgets would be inoperative. The number of times I have seen steam-chest pressure gauges out of action is legion: there were power-operated fire-doors that would not work, and such like. But I shall always remember the comment of an old friend whose footplate riding has been even more world-wide than my own, and who once said how good it was to be once more on a Great Western engine where everything in the cab worked! I am afraid that until hearing this remark I had been inclined to take such 'working' for granted on the GWR. It was an eloquent testimony to the workmanship put into all these important fittings.

To quote Cook once again: 'At a period prior to World War II there was a considerable body of industrial opinion who regarded the railway workshops as a collection of primitive and antiquated machines and quite beyond the pale of making any contribution to wartime needs of production. Possibly this arose from the fact that by statute railway workshops have to stand aloof from the outside engineering industry, to deal with their own internal requirements only. The condition of their machine tools was probably well known among the machine tool makers who had derived considerable benefit during the slump years from the railway's practice of keeping equipment up to date; but industry in general and officialdom in particular had a complete misconception of the wide range of capacity necessary to provide for the mechanical and productive needs of a great railway.'

While Cook in his presidential address was naturally speaking in general terms, his remarks applied with redoubled emphasis to the Great Western, where his own contribution to the situation was no small one. For those readers who are particularly interested in the details of workshop practice I can strongly recommend a two-part article contributed by Cook himself to the 14 and 21 August issues of *The Railway Gazette* in 1936 on the 'Machining of a Locomotive Valve Gear'. This related to the 'Hall' class, and was a most comprehensive and fascinating survey. That the example chosen for description, in the year of grace 1936, was the Stephenson link motion, is evidence of the fact that this valve gear was the cornerstone of GWR standard practice in steam distribution. On this point, by way of introduction, Cook writes: 'Much might be written concerning the relative merits of valve gears of the Stephenson or Walschaerts type. A good layout can be obtained with the former type on engines of this cylinder arrangement, which provides easy accessibility together with good wearing qualities. The bulk of the gear lies between the frames in a space not required for other parts, and it also has the benefit of leaving the piston cross-heads, coupling and connecting rods free from valve gear attachments and, therefore, removable without any further dismantling.'

Readers of the railway press of the day who studied articles of this kind, would gain some insight into the quality of the machinery and work then characteristic of Swindon, and Cook in his presidential address referred particularly to the tool room, which services all the production shops.

'During World War II,' he continued, 'the cloak was removed and the railway workshops became open doors for all who wanted help. But it took a little time to pierce the cloud. At the end of exploratory visits by the productive ministries, the officials began to scratch their heads and exclaim: "We are on the wrong line—we have been looking to find out what you can produce—we should have been seeking what you cannot." One official of the Ministry of Aircraft Production exclaimed: "You have the finest toolroom outside the aircraft industry." Later during the war he knew that there was hardly an aircraft factory which was not using ground thread taps produced in that tool room.'

The equipment of Swindon Works was a resounding tribute to the great personal interest Collett himself took in the manufacturing methods, but no less to the scope he gave to Hannington and Cook. On the outbreak of war Collett had already reached the age of sixty-eight and he continued in office for another two critical years. Hannington died in 1937, while still in office, having been locomotive works manager since 1922. He was succeeded immediately by Cook, and thus the continuity of practice continued without the slightest intermission. I cannot close the mention of these changes in personnel without referring to the *personalia*, if I may call it so, of the 'Hall' class locomotives. As successive batches of these engines were built considerable difficulty was found in providing suitable names. A particular engine, much featured in official photographs at Swindon was No 5930 *Hannington Hall*. I have never succeeded in finding, in a gazetteer, where this 'stately home' is, but it was somewhat naturally in favour with the works management. It was at about this same time that a wag in the drawing office suggested that another engine of the class might be named *Fred Hall*—after F. C. Hall, the very popular outdoor assistant and locomotive running superintendent!

Collett himself shrank from any form of publicity, and for this reason he missed an outstanding opportunity to advance the prestige of Great Western locomotives in 1935. With the advance in design practice on the northern lines the pre-eminence of Swindon in the eyes of railway enthusiasts was beginning to slip. Eight years had passed since the introduction of the 'Kings' and the fact that there had been an extensive return to 'Castle' building was in certain quarters taken as an indication that the 'Kings' were not entirely successful. To fall back upon a design of 1923 seemed to some people a confession that the fount of new ideas had run dry at Swindon. Then came the year 1935—not only the Silver Jubilee year of His Majesty King George V, but also the centenary of

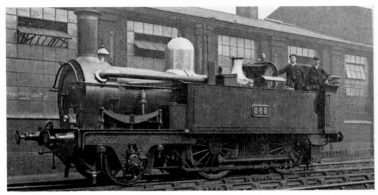

Page 177. (above) *One of the Armstrong 'Metro' tanks, No 968. A total of 110 was built, and by 1922 only 19 had been scrapped;* (centre) *outside-framed 0–6–0 tank engine No 740 originally built in 1873, and shown here as rebuilt with pannier tanks;* (below) *one of the Collett 0–4–2 tanks, No 1423 at Fishguard Harbour in 1947*

Page 178. (above) *2–6–2 tank engine No 4548 leaving Kingswear with an up train, including at rear two through carriages for Paddington; (below) Kingsbridge branch train approaching Gara Bridge: 2–6–2 tank engine No 5551*

the Act of Incorporation of the GWR. What an opportunity for a dual celebration! In various overseas countries streamlining was being applied to locomotives and high-speed railcars, and certain members of the locomotive committee of the Great Western Board suggested to Collett that it would be a good idea to have some streamlined locomotives, to show that the company was 'with it' in respect of this ultra-modern trend. Had this suggestion been played for what it was worth the Great Western could have scored another 'first' in public eyes. It would not have made any difference to the performance of the locomotives, except perhaps to detract from their accessibility for essential maintenance; but just think what might have been done for publicity in centenary year, with fully streamlined locomotives, and possibly a still higher speed record between Swindon and Paddington! It could easily have been done with appropriate prior organisation.

But Collett treated the suggestion with ill-concealed ridicule. I have told elsewhere how an office boy was sent out to buy some plasticine, and how Collett took a paperweight model of a 'King', rubbed some of the plasticine on the smokebox door, produced fairing behind the chimney, safety valve cover, and a slightly wedge-shaped front to the cab, and then sent the model into the drawing office with instructions for a 'King' and a 'Castle' to be 'dolled-up' like that. And so *King Henry VII* and *Manorbier Castle* became the first 'streamlined' engines to run in Great Britain. The great chance was lost, and in September 1935 the emergence of *Silver Link* from Doncaster Works with its sensational appearance, and still more sensational performance, stole the limelight from the Great Western so completely that it was not to return until the old company had ceased to exist, and an LNER man was largely responsible for restoring the one-time eminence of Swindon in the eyes of the railway world at large.

I have written that the record of 1932 with the 'Cheltenham Flyer' could easily have been surpassed had there been a real desire to do so. The first locomotives to be built new at Swindon with the optical system of frame and axlebox alignment were the 1934 batch of 'Castles', numbered from 5023 to 5032, and onwards. These engines immediately gained a reputation for exceptionally fine performances. I have already referred in the previous chapter to a run of my own with engine No 5025, *Chirk Castle* on the Cheltenham Flyer, while No 5023, *Brecon Castle* has the honour of working the train very nearly to time with a load of 435 tons—*four hundred and thirty-five tons!* Again 5039 *Rhuddlan Castle*, on a journey made without any special preparation, beat the times of the world record run over the major part of the distance between Swindon and Paddington. These indeed were locomotives of precision, and one would dearly have liked to have seen what they could have done if really pressed for another world record. But the urge to produce spectacular running seems to have slipped away from the Great Western Railway after the departure of Sir Felix Pole from the general managership at Paddington. It was he who inspired all the initial publicity with the 'Kings', and with the rapid advance in speed achievement by the northern lines the great intrinsic merit of Great Western locomotives was reflected more in their splendid maintenance and running costs, rather than in any advance upon the very high standards of speed that had been set by 1932.

CHAPTER 12

Wartime Transition
Collett to Hawksworth

THE declaration of war on Nazi Germany by Great Britain and France on 3 September 1939, following the onslaught upon Poland, did not prove so immediate a line of demarcation for the locomotive department of the GWR as it did for many other British institutions. For one thing there were urgent tasks to be done that required all the resources of the department as it then existed. All the same, the year 1939 provides a good milestone at which to take stock of the locomotive position, and statistics at the end of the year provide an interesting study. Then the total numbers of the various wheel arrangements were as shown in Table 31.

TABLE 31

Tender engines		Tank engines	
Type	Total	Type	Total
4–6–0	554	2–8–2T	54
4–4–0	93	2–8–0T	141
2–8–0	173	2–6–2T	441
2–6–0	271	2–4–0T	27
2–4–0	3	0–8–2T	1
0–6–0	253	0–6–2T	406
		0–6–0T	1152
		0–4–2T	111
		0–4–0T	20

So far as individual classes were concerned, the 'Grange' class of 4–6–0 had, during the year, been brought up to its ultimately full strength of eighty engines by the building of Nos 6860-79 at Swindon. The 'Manor' class 4–6–0 had been brought up to a total of twenty, by addition of Nos 7812-19, while seven additional 'Dukedogs' Nos 3222-28 made a total of twenty-nine engines of that class. The replacement of the 4063 to 4072 series of 'Abbey' class 4–6–0s by 'Castles' was proceeding, and by the end of the year only No 4067 *Tintern Abbey* remained in traffic as a 'Star'. There were of course the first two engines of the 'Abbey' series, Nos 4061-2, which were never converted to 'Castles'. During the year 1939 *Evesham Abbey*, *Llanthony Abbey*, *Westminster Abbey* and *Neath Abbey* re-appeared as 'Castles' numbered 5085, 5088, 5089 and 5090 respectively. The '5013' series of 'Castles' was completed by the construction of new engines 5078 to 5082, and 5093 to 5097. During the year another twelve of the improved 2–8–0s were built, bringing the number of the '28XX' and '38XX' up to a total of 114, and another ten of the light branch 0–6–0s of the '2251' class were added. Among the tank engines the largest addition was fifty more panniers of the '57XX' class.

One of the most important immediate effects of the war was the setting aside of 100 'Dean Goods' 0–6–0s for overseas service. To replace them it was originally arranged for the loan to the GWR of forty 0–6–0s each from the LMS and the LNER, while twenty Great Western engines that had been condemned were repaired, and reinstated on the active list. These latter included a number of older 0–6–0s, and pannier tanks of nineteenth-century vintage. There were also three '31XX' series of 2–6–2 tanks, and two 'Bulldog' class 4–4–0s. The 'Dean Goods' allocated to the War Department were renumbered, painted black, and fitted with the Westinghouse brake. But the inclusion of the Flaman speed recording apparatus, as then coming into extensive use in France, seemed a totally unnecessary elaboration for locomotives intended for secondary if important duties in the war zone. It was a tribute to the quality of Great Western locomotive design and maintenance, even of old engines, that some of those selected for this allocation had given overseas service in World War I.

One of the first duties that fell to the lot of 'Great Western Steam' in World War II, or to be strictly correct just before it began, was the working of the evacuation specials from London. This operation had been planned in the most complete detail well beforehand; but even so, seeing that the order authorising the movement was not given until Thursday 31 August, it was remarkable that the first special left Ealing Broadway at 8.30am on the following morning, and that no fewer than thirty-four trains were run, at approximately ten-minute intervals, on that one day! In view of the historic nature of the movement it is worth setting on record the actual locomotives involved in this 'errand of mercy'! The shorter distance trains destined for Reading, Oxford and stations between, also stations on the Berks and Hants line, were worked by 2–6–2 tanks, and the engines involved were 6112, 6120, 6121, 6141, 6143, 6146, 6149, 6153, 6156 and 6169. Three trains were hauled by standard Moguls Nos 4365, 6386 and 8338, while the remainder were taken by express passenger and mixed traffic 4–6–0s as follows:

'Star' class:

4015	*Knight of St John*
4019	*Knight Templar*
4020	*Knight Commander*
4040	*Queen Boadicea*
4050	*Princess Alice*

'Castle' class:

4082	*Windsor Castle*
4090	*Dorchester Castle*
4099	*Kilgerran Castle*
5022	*Wigmore Castle*
5024	*Carew Castle*
5029	*Nunney Castle*
5066	*Wardour Castle**
5079	*Lydford Castle**
5086	*Viscount Horne*

'King' class:

| 6029 | *King Edward VIII* |

183

'Hall' class:

5955   *Garth Hall*
5973   *Rolleston Hall*

'Grange' class:

6822   *Manton Grange*
6846   *Ruckley Grange*
6873   *Caradoc Grange*
6876   *Kingsland Grange*

* names carried in 1939

In the stock returns for the fifty-two weeks ended 9 December 1939 construction of new locomotives of the 'Hall' class had proceeded up to No 5990, but additions were still being made, if slowly, and by the end of 1940 the serial numbers had crept up to 6910. In April 1941 with the completion of engine No 6915 *Mursley Hall* the practice of naming ceased as a wartime economy measure. As the possessor of a nameplate off one of the earlier Great Western 4–6–0s I can testify to the weight of solid metal incorporated in them! Construction of these most useful and appropriate general service engines continued at intervals during 1941 and 1942, also of the largest variety of pannier tanks and 2–8–0 freight engines. The lining out of express passenger locomotives was discontinued, as repairs were executed at Swindon; copper caps on the chimneys, and safety valve covers were painted over, while all repainted engines other than 'Stars', 'Castles' and 'Kings' were mostly painted black.

In July 1941 following the retirement of Mr Collett certain changes took place in the top management of the locomotive department consequent upon the appointment of F. W. Hawksworth as chief mechanical engineer. F. C. Hall became principal assistant, and he was succeeded by W. N. Pellow, as outdoor assistant and locomotive running superintendent. K. J. Cook and H. Randle remained in their posts as works managers of the locomotive and carriage works respectively. F. C. Mattingley was chief draughtsman, and A. W. J. Dymond, appointed as an assistant to the chief mechanical engineer, was entrusted with some of the most important developments of the later years. In the immediate future, however, the exigencies of wartime control precluded any actual development as such, and Swindon works undertook the building of a number of LMS standard 2–8–0 mineral engines of Stanier design, under instructions from the Ministry of War Transport.

I had the pleasure and privilege of Mr Hawksworth's friendship, and heard at first hand some of the problems with which he was faced. He granted me many opportunities for observing the work of his locomotives from the footplate during a particularly interesting and difficult period in Great Western locomotive history. One can well appreciate that Collett, approaching the age of three score years and ten felt little inclination to change locomotive design, or to consider adapting it to the rapidly changing conditions, and to the end of his time the old traditions that he had inherited from Churchward were continued in their entirety. Hawksworth on the other hand was well enough aware of the need for some change, if for no other reason than the rapidly deteriorating quality of fuel supplies. It was not so much that coal was consistently bad; it was the day-to-day variation that so bedevilled locomotive working. Taken all round the Great Western drivers and their firemen did remarkably well, adapting themselves from day to day to the stuff loaded on to their tenders. As I have explained earlier in this book there was nothing in the way of fixed allocation of engines to crews. The links at the majority of sheds mostly had such a diversity of turns that one did not even keep to the same *class* of engine. It was the engine that went with the job.

In 1941, when Hawksworth took over, the Great Western was standing entirely alone in its use of no more than a moderate degree of superheat. With good coal and expert driving and firing the Churchward boilers and their direct derivatives gave magnificent results; but once adverse circumstances led to a deterioration in the steaming 'they'd had it', to use a colloquialism. Hawksworth decided at once that for new locomotives a higher degree of superheat must be incorporated, and this was applied first on a new batch of 'Halls', construction of which began in 1944. These engines, known as the

'6959' class, had for the first time since its design was finalised a modified version of the No 1 standard boiler; the superheater was of a new type, and the heating surfaces as compared with the original were as shown in Table 32.

TABLE 32

Boiler	Standard No 1	'Hall' '6959' class
Heating surfaces sq ft		
Tubes	1687	1582.6
Firebox	155	154.9
Superheater elements	263	314.6
Total	2105	2052.1

It is true that during the years 1914-19 a total of 108 boilers with Swindon No 3 superheaters were built with 112 elements, instead of 84, and giving 330sq ft of heating surface; but this type was not standardised. In the '6959' class the traditional Swindon No 3 superheater was abandoned in favour of a new design that was similar to the Schmidt, but had the regulator valve incorporated in the header as in previous practice. Another break with old traditions was in the bogie and engine main framing, and in the method of supporting the smokebox and cylinders. Previous practice, used on all the two-cylinder standard engines was to cast the saddle supporting the front end of the boiler integrally with the cylinders, in two halves bolted together in the engine centre line. The cylinders were carried on forged steel extensions bolted to the main frames. This design originated with the earliest Churchward 4–6–0s. In the '6959' class Hawksworth adopted the more usual arrangement of carrying the main plate frames through to the front buffer beam. The cylinders were cast separately from the saddle, and the latter was formed as part of a fabricated assembly that also provided a stiffener between the frames at the point where the cylinders were attached. The bar-frame bogies of the Swindon–de Glehn type were abandoned in favour of a simple plate-frame design, with the load transmitted to the axle boxes through four laminated springs.

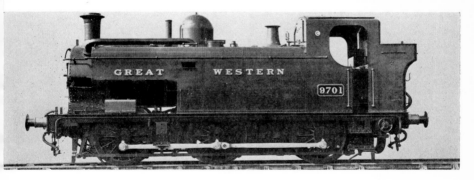

Page 187. (above) *A standard 2–8–0 freight engine, oil-fired No 2872;* (upper centre) Haberfield Hall, *oil-fired, and temporarily renumbered 3955;* (lower centre) *the first oil-fired 'Castle' No 5091* Cleeve Abbey *with small tender;* (below) *one of the new standard pannier tanks with condensing gear, No 9701*

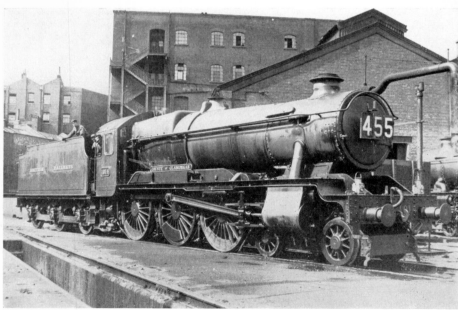

Page 188. (above) *4–6–0 No 5046* Earl Cawdor *in first post-war style of painting;* (below) *new two-cylinder 4–6–0 No 1014* County of Glamorgan *at Ranelagh Bridge yard*

The new engines were an immediate success and while not exhibiting any marked superiority over the existing 'Halls' in optimum conditions were notably free in steaming, particularly when fuel was not of the best. They had the standard 4,000-gallon tender, and when first turned out were painted plain black and unnamed. At the time these engines took the road the war situation was such that victory seemed only a matter of time, and thoughts could be directed towards post-war reconstruction and development. The thoughts of any chief mechanical engineer would naturally have turned to provision of power for express passenger traffic. On the Southern O. V. S. Bulleid under the cloak of a 'mixed-traffic' designation had built some new 'Pacific' engines of high capacity. On the LNER Edward Thompson had produced his ungainly prototype 'Pacifics' by rebuilding the Gresley 'P2' class 2–8–2s, and the LMS had already some first rate 'Pacifics' in the Stanier 'Duchess' class. Hawksworth also considered a 'Pacific', but I have told elsewhere how what could well have proved a remarkable design was stillborn. I will do no more than set down what were understood to be the basic dimensions alongside Pacifics of Stanier, Bulleid, and E. Thompson (see Table 33).

TABLE 33

BRITISH PACIFICS: ACTUAL AND PROPOSED

Railway		LMS	SOUTHERN	LNER	GWR
Designer		Stanier	Bulleid	Thompson	Hawksworth
Class		'Duchess'	'Merchant Navy'	'A2/2'	Not built
Cylinders: number		4	3	3	4
diameter	in	$16\frac{1}{2}$	18	20	$16\frac{1}{4}$
stroke	in	28	24	26	28
Coupled wheel diameter	ft in	6–9	6–2	6–2	6–3
Boiler pressure	psi	250	280	225	280
Nominal Tractive Effort	lb	40,000	37,500	40,318	46,800

189

L

Although authority to build this engine was not forthcoming immediately Hawksworth did not abandon the idea entirely, and when a further batch of 4–6–0 mixed traffic locomotives was authorised in 1945 he took the opportunity to incorporate two features that were intended for the 'Pacific', namely 6ft 3in coupled wheels, and a boiler pressure of 280lb per square inch. I believe the original intention was to use the 'Castle' boiler, but the weight came out too heavy and a new design was worked out, using the tools that were on hand at Swindon from the building of the standard LMS 2–8–0 freight engines for the Ministry of War Transport. The variation in the boilers of these two locomotive types was remarkably small (Table 34).

TABLE 34

A BOILER COMPARISON

		LMS	GWR
Class		'8F'	'1000'
Barrel	ft in		
max diameter		5–8⅜	5–8⅜
min diameter		5–0	5–0
length		12–3$\frac{9}{16}$	12–7$\frac{3}{16}$
Heating surfaces	sq ft		
tubes		1479	1545
firebox		171	169
superheater		230	265
total		1880	1979
Grate area	sq ft	28.65	28.84

The new Great Western mixed traffic 4–6–0 had the standard 18½in by 30in cylinders, mounted as in the '6959' series of 'Halls', but the higher boiler pressure put the nominal tractive effort up to 32,580lb. The first engine of the class, No 1000, had a twin-orifice blastpipe and chimney, though she was the only one to have this feature originally. A new all-welded design of tender, with entirely smooth sides was introduced on this class. The water capacity remainder at 4,000 gallons, but the coal capacity was increased from 6 to 7 tons. The total weight of these new tenders when fully loaded was

49 tons, as compared to the 46.7 tons of those attached to the 'Hall', 'Castle' and 'King' class engines. To the delight of all Great Western enthusiasts the new engines were turned out fully lined in the old style, and the copper chimney top on No 1000 looked tremendous. The first new engines of the class were unnamed; but then the names of the old '38XX' class 4–4–0s were revived and No 1000 became *County of Middlesex*.

It cannot unfortunately be said that these engines were an immediate success. They were put into express passenger service in the same links as 'Castles', at Bristol, Wolverhampton, Newton Abbot and Laira sheds, and although much of the work I personally experienced was very good, there were many instances of indifferent steaming. This could, in certain cases, be attributed to inexperience on the part of the men, and in 1945 there was not the same opportunity for nursing a new design into its stride that had been customary in earlier days on the GWR. But whereas the modified 'Halls' had been universally welcomed for their freedom in steaming, the 'Counties' at first got the reputation of being rather 'touchy'. There was also much criticism of the fore and aft surging action they imparted to the train. The 'Saints' did this at times, but never to such a pronounced degree as the 'Counties'. They were at first prohibited from running over the Midland line between Yate and Standish, and could not therefore be used on the Wolverhampton–West of England expresses via the North Warwick line. All these were happily no more than teething troubles, and in due course the 'Counties' settled down to do some really excellent work. They had the traditional 'punch' of all the Great Western two-cylinder engines in starting away, and while they could never equal the 'Castles' in free running at really high speed their workings were rationalised on to the routes most suitable to their characteristics.

Most of my own earliest experiences with these engines was on the Bristol main line, and the majority were good, without any approach to brilliance. But on the footplate I had some very interesting runs that showed both the strength and weakness of the class. The first of these latter was obtained in unexpected circumstances. I had a footplate pass to ride the Penzance–Wolverhampton express, on a summer Saturday.

With the Cornish part of the train of nine coaches we did well with a 'Star' from Plymouth to Exeter, but then, with six more coaches added, and a Stafford Road 'Castle' that was not in the best of condition, we were soon in dire trouble with a gross load of 525 tons behind the tender. The most serious fault with No 5015 *Kingswear Castle* was a leak in the vacuum system, which made the cross-head pump partially ineffective and made it necessary to use the small ejector to keep the brakes off. This was a drain on the steam raising capacity of an ailing engine, and we were soon losing time hand over fist. The inspector who was riding with me threw out a message as we passed Cullompton, and when we arrived at Taunton a couple of fitters were waiting to try and locate the fault on the brake and to try to remedy it. It was a lengthy business, and in the end quite abortive, and so a 'County' class engine which was standing ready to take a succeeding semi-fast train to Bristol was commandeered.

From the operating point of view the afternoon's proceedings were somewhat misjudged. With such a load as 525 tons the train would have required double-heading throughout from Bristol to Wolverhampton, and a 'Star', No 4053 *Princess Alexandra* had already been detailed for the job and was standing ready at Temple Meads. Far more time was lost at Taunton trying to patch up the vacuum system on No 5015 than would have been lost even with that poor engine in continuing to Bristol; and then with another engine coupled on ahead the vacuum trouble would have ceased and that lame duck could have been got back to her home shed. To crown all there was another major difficulty which the inspector riding with me did not appreciate. He was a Newton Abbot man and evidently did not know the 'Counties' were prohibited from running between Yate and Standish; and no one at Taunton thought to advise Bristol of the engine that had been substituted for the disabled 'Castle'. Consequently when we arrived at Bristol the train was headed by an engine that could go no further, and Bath Road shed had the unwelcome task of finding a suitable engine at a moment's notice to partner the 'Star' No 4053 which was ready and waiting. The driver who had come up from Exeter was a Bristol man, who was not concerned with what happened afterwards! As it turned out I was the only person who derived any satisfaction out of that ill-starred affair—with an interesting and useful piece of footplate running with a 'County' in my notebook.

County of Cardigan was the engine, with a train of fifteen coaches, 473 tons tare, 525 tons full. There was a very severe slack for relaying at Dunball, but we got going well after this, and passed Yatton, 32.8 miles from Taunton, in 37½min, or 33min net. The cut-off was 20 per cent and regulator opened just wide enough to bring the main valve into operation. This was enough to sustain 64-5mph on level track. Pressure was maintained steadily at 275-280lb per square inch at first, but there was a slight falling off to about 260 after about half an hour's running. On the rise to Flax Bourton cut-off was increased first to 22 and then 25 per cent. Net time over the 44.8 miles from Taunton to Bristol was 47min start to stop, an excellent average speed of 57.2mph, seeing that the engine had been commandeered at a moment's notice, and had not originally been prepared for a duty as strenuous as this.

On the Bristol main line I had a number of good runs, and the log is appended in Table 35 of an experience I had on the footplate of No 1014 *County of Glamorgan* on the 9.0am up from Temple Meads. It was a Saturday, and we were badly delayed by congestion of traffic inwards from Maidenhead, but until then we had run well, with the engine steaming freely. During the spell of undelayed running the boiler pressure lay between 245 and 270lb per square inch with the engine working in 25 per cent cut-off with the regulator just opened on to the second valve. But it was a very different story on the return trip with the 1.15pm also non-stop be–tween Paddington and Bath. The fireman had dug down to some dreadful coal that seemed little better than dust, with a liberal admixture of ovoids. This was hardly the stuff to make any engine steam, let alone one of a class that could be some-what touchy at times. Again we suffered a number of severe delays en route; but these really helped the fireman! At each pause in the steaming, while we were running under adverse signals or momentarily at rest, he could rally the boiler, so that the driver could get away with almost full pressure. But directly we settled down to steady fast running, at slightly better than scheduled speed, the demand began to beat the

TABLE 35

WESTERN REGION: BATH–PADDINGTON

Load: 13 coaches, 432 tons tare, 470 tons full
Engine: 1014 *County of Glamorgan*

Distance miles		Sch min	Actual min sec		Speeds mph
0.0	BATH	0	0	00	—
2.3	Bathampton		4	27	46
5.0	Box		7	50	52
8.6	Corsham		13	07	32½
12.9	CHIPPENHAM	18	17	52	64
19.2	Dauntsey		23	39	68
24.0	Wootton Bassett		28	53	50½ (min)
29.6	SWINDON	37	34	35	65
41.4	Uffington		44	16	69½
46.6	Wantage Road		49	27	72
53.8	DIDCOT	61½	55	40	70½
60.3	*South Stoke Box*		61	25	69
—			sigs	pw	
70.9	READING	78	75	58	
75.9	Twyford	83	82	20	62 (max)
—			many	checks	
106.9	PADDINGTON	119	131	45	

Net time 109 minutes

boiler, and down came the pressure once more, and we were sometimes down as low as 170lb per square inch.

One of the most interesting runs I had on the Bristol route came one summer's evening on the 5p.m. down—again non-stop to Bath. We had engine No 1011 *County of Chester* and made a normal run as far as Didcot; but then the fireman, looking back, spotted what he thought was smoke coming from the leading coach. They stopped at Steventon for examination, and sure enough found that an axlebox on the leading coach was running hot. There was nothing for it but to detach that coach. Passengers and their luggage had to be transferred to other parts of the train, and the coach parked in the small station yard that then existed at Steventon. All this took a considerable time, especially the separating of buck–eye couplers between the first and second coaches—a strenuous operation in which the travelling ticket collector and the fireman participated. Once this was done, however, Driver Grainger made a determined effort to regain what time he could, and I logged the fine run set out in Table 36.

TABLE 36

WESTERN REGION: STEVENTON–BATH

Load: 342 tons tare, 370 tons full
Engine: 1011 County of Chester

Distance Miles		Actual min sec		Speeds mph
0.0	Steventon*	0	00	—
3.8	Wantage Road	5	44	57
9.9	Uffington	11	27	70
14.9	Shrivenham	15	56	66
20.7	SWINDON	21	20	eased
26.3	Wootton Bassett	26	14	71½
31.1	Dauntsey	30	14	74
37.4	CHIPPENHAM	35	49	65
41.7	Corsham	39	38	69
45.3	Box	42	40	72
49.2	*Milepost 105¾*	46	07	
50.3	BATH	47	50	

*Stop near West signal box

The engine was eased prior to running through Swindon and Chippenham, but was pressed to vigorous accelerations afterwards. The speeds of 70mph at Uffington and 69 at Corsham were notable on gradually rising gradients.

To see the 'Counties' at their best, however, one had to ride the north road from Wolverhampton. While a number of expresses on the Birmingham route from Paddington went forward from Wolverhampton with considerably reduced loads by the detaching of dining cars, there were some like the 11.10am from Paddington that took their full load forward to Shrewsbury; and there were some up workings that were similarly loaded. For the first five years, or so, after the end of World War II some of these trains were loading regularly to between 450 and 500 tons gross, and presented no small tasks in haulage over the sharply graded line between Wolverhampton and Wellington. Fortunately the gradients are not very long, but even so stretches of 1 in 110, and 1 in 120, when they extend to several miles, cannot be discounted with such loads as those carried on the heaviest trains. The 'Counties', in the very able hands of the Stafford Road No 2 link, were ideal for such a task. They could develop a high power output at medium speed in the characteristic style of the Swindon two-cylinder engines, and then if the boiler pressure had been run down a little in making a big effort uphill the situation could be quickly recovered downhill. I had many opportunities of observing the running over this route, several times from the footplate, and with the help of much additional data put at my disposal by Messrs A. V. Goodyear and J. C. Keyte I was able to make a very comprehensive assessment of 'County' performance. Our combined records included work of 'Saints', 'Stars' and 'Castles', and in these particular duties I can say without any hesitation that the 'Counties' were pre-eminent.

I have tabulated details of four runs between Wolverhampton and Wellington, and to appreciate these the gradients need to be considered. Although Wellington lies at a considerably lower level than Wolverhampton the steep descent from Hollinswood Tunnel could not be used for fast running, and the aggregate gradient between Stafford Road Junction and Hollinswood is slightly adverse. But the main feature of this stretch of line is the Shifnal bank, with 1.9 miles at 1 in 150 and 2.8 miles at 1 in 100. Even though this was preceeded by a sharp descent from Albrighton, such a bank needs careful working with loads of 450 to 500 tons. The first run detailed in Table 37 was a magnificent example of what the 'Saints' could still do in years just after World War II. Except in the lower minimum speed at Hollinswood its running is barely distinguishable from the far more powerful 'Counties'. *County of Radnor,* on run No 3 drew ahead of No 1029 by a most vigorous start, and made the fastest time of all to Hollinswood; but the honours, if any are to be bestowed, must go to *County of Worcester* in the fourth column for her remarkable climb

TABLE 37

WESTERN REGION: WOLVERHAMPTON–WELLINGTON

Run No		1	2	3	4
Engine No		2915	1029	1025	1029
Engine Name		*Saint Bartholomew*	*County of Worcester*	*County of Radnor*	*County of Worcester*
Load tons E/F		414/445	427/460	429/460	458/500
Distance miles		Actual min sec	Actual min sec	Actual min sec	Actual min sec
0.0	WOLVERHAMPTON	0 00	0 00	0 00	0 00
1.3	*Stafford Road Junction*	3 11	3 20	3 01	3 11
4.7	Codsall	7 10	7 05	6 51	7 09
7.7	Albrighton	10 06	9 58	9 42	10 04
9.2	Cosford	11 18	11 10	10 55	11 21
12.5	Shifnal	13 58	13 51	13 36	14 10
15.4	*Hollinswood Box*	17 42	17 35	17 00	17 45
16.6	Oakengates	19 10	19 03	18 24	19 13
—				sigs	—
19.6	WELLINGTON	23 00	22 25	22 52	23 16
Speeds	mph				
Codsall	(max)	57	62	61½	58
Cosford	(max)	78	80	78	73½
Hollinswood	(min)	39	41	43	43

to Hollinswood with a 500-ton train, from the lowest maximum speed of any at Cosford. I calculate that this engine was developing 1,500 drawbar horsepower at the foot of the Shifnal bank, and 1,400 at the top.

CHAPTER 13

GWR to BR (WR):
The Final Hawksworth Years

HAWKSWORTH'S developments towards the use of a higher degree of superheat were not confined to the two-cylinder engines. In 1947 construction of the 'Castle' class 4–6–0s was resumed, beginning with No 5098 *Clifford Castle*. The pioneer of this new series was the third to bear this name. It had first been displaced from No 5046, when that engine was renamed *Earl Cawdor*, and secondly from No 5071, which in 1940 was renamed *Spitfire*. The modified boiler and superheated proportion as compared with those of the original '4073' and '5013' classes may be studied in Table 38.

TABLE 38

'CASTLE' BOILERS

Class		4073-5013	5098
Small tubes	number	197	170
Flues	number	14	21
Heating surfaces	sq ft		
tubes		1858	1800
firebox		163	164
superheater		263	313
Grate area	sq ft	29.4	29.4

The first two engines of the '5098' class retained the hydrostatic lubricators hitherto standard but all the subsequent engines had mechanical lubricators. The running inspectors reckoned that Nos 5098 and 5099 were, when new, the best 'Castles' ever, combining the freedom of running characteristics of the class as a whole, with that little 'extra' derived from a higher degree of superheat. The engines numbered from 7000 upwards, though very powerful, were not regarded as quite so fast at first, and this was perhaps a psychological reaction to engines on which the driver could not regulate the oil supply himself. In my own experience, including several hundreds of miles on her footplate, *Clifford Castle* was indeed a grand engine. The earliest units of the '5098' class up to No 7007 had tenders of the previous standard 4,000-gallon type, but from No 7008 upwards the new straight-sided tender, as introduced on the 'Counties', was used.

In the meantime the coal situation on the railway as a whole had deteriorated to an alarming degree, and ironically enough nowhere worse than in South Wales. When the prosperity of that region in years before World War I is recalled —a prosperity almost entirely based upon indigenous mineral riches—it would seem utterly incredible that in 1946-7 locomotives in South Wales should be running on coal of very poor quality imported from the USA. I have the most vivid recollections of travelling in a train from Merthyr Tydfil down to Cardiff, 'hauled' by one of the '56XX' class 0-6-2 tank engines, which was steaming so badly on American coal that we had to stop in mid-section several times for the fireman to walk the length of the train releasing the brakes by hand. The loss of time became so serious that I began to fear the loss of my connection to London at Cardiff, but fortunately Pontypridd produced a Taff Vale 'A' class 0-6-2 tank to pilot our sorely tried '56XX'. The former engine was in top class form, and no more time was lost. It was this general situation, of which my own experience was no isolated incident, that led to the Great Western experiment with oil firing, and it is certainly significant that the first locomotives to be equipped were 2-8-0s engaged in the heavy mineral traffic between Llanelly and Severn Tunnel Junction.

So far as the locomotives themselves were concerned this was no hasty improvisation. The modified fireboxes were well designed and gave very good service, and following the first experience with the '28XX' class a number of 'Hall' and 'Castle' class 4-6-0s were converted. I had some very good runs with these, and while a few of them were kept on the

London–Bristol main line, where they were conveniently on hand for observation from headquarters at Swindon, the intention was to make Cornwall an oil-fired area, and so reduce the cost of hauling coal to that 'outpost'. Alas for any well thought out planning by one of the former railway companies! In the fuel crisis that broke over the heads of Mr Attlee's government in the winter of 1946-7 someone in authority evidently heard of the Great Western success with oil firing and hailed it as a national inspiration. Despite the conditions of austerity then prevailing, finance was made available for the conversion of large numbers of locomotives on other railways. That was not all. Oil firing cannot be adopted without adequate servicing facilities, and the erection of fuelling plants was put in hand at many centres in Great Britain. Only when some three million pounds of public money had been spent did another government department point out that we did not possess the necessary foreign exchange to purchase the oil! Many of the fuelling plants were never used at all. The bungling politicians who between them blundered into this most culpable situation were, of course, never brought to task, and the well-conceived Great Western plan for application of oil-firing in certain defined and limited areas foundered in the national *débâcle*.

I had some interesting runs with the oil-fired engines. In Cornwall I heard No 5079 *Lysander* referred to as the 'flagship' of the oil-fired fleet. She was a very good engine, and steamed with a consistency that I had rarely seen previously with coal-fired locomotives. But with heavily loaded trains she displayed the weakness of the four-cylinder 4–6–0s when slogging at slow speed up the severe banks. As a breed they were never so good as the two-cylinder engines in such circumstances, and with trains well below the onerous maximum of 420 tons tare *Lysander* had to be worked very hard to keep time—in fact she generally lost a little on the uphill sections and regained it on the generously-timed downhill lengths. This was nothing to do with oil-firing. On the contrary, the consistency of the steaming allowed the drivers to pound the engine without any fear of running her short of steam. But the details of the engine working in Tables 39 and 40 are enough to show the extent to which she was opened out.

TABLE 39

DOWN CORNISH RIVIERA EXPRESS
Plymouth–Truro

Engine: 'Castle' class 4–6–0 No 5079 *Lysander*
Load: 365 tons gross trailing
Cut-off ranges:

Plymouth–Par	24 to 40 per cent
Par–Truro	26 to 45 per cent

TABLE 40

UP CORNISH RIVIERA EXPRESS
Truro–Plymouth

Engine: 'Castle' class 4–6–0 No 5079 *Lysander*
Load: 360 tons gross trailing
Cut-off ranges:

Truro–Par	30 to 35 per cent
Par–Plymouth	26 to 40 per cent

Hawksworth was in process of carrying his developments in superheating still further when the nationalisation of the railways took place in January 1948. The '6959' series of 'Halls' and the '5098' series of 'Castles' represented no more than a moderate advance upon the original proportions, but there were no half measures about the changes made to engine No 6022 *King Edward III*. This had a four-row superheater of new design with the changes in dimensions from the original shown in Table 41.

As modified 'she'—if one may retain the traditional feminine gender for an engine named after such a redoubtable monarch as he who created the Order of the Garter—was a grand engine. I was privileged to see her running on the Swindon stationary plant, and in so doing met for the first time the inimitable Sam Ell, then engineer in charge of testing and experimental work. But everything the Great Western had been doing in the development of its steam locomotive practice was very much slowed down by the onset of nationalisation, and I must defer reference to the actual working of engine No 6022 until I have dealt with the interesting series of Interchange Trials initiated by the newly formed Railway

Executive. To railway enthusiasts the prospects of large scale exchanges between the locomotives of the former independent railway companies was fascinating beyond measure. But before a single test train had set out it could well have seemed to an outsider that the dice was loaded against the Great Western. For it was only over the former LNER lines that Great Western locomotives were accepted. They were precluded from running on all LMS lines and on the Southern. Consequently there was to be no chance of seeing how a 'King' would climb Shap, or Honiton; no chance of a 'Hall' tackling the lengthy climbs to Peak Forest, in the course of a St Pancras–Manchester run. There was some compensation in this latter case, however, in that a 'Hall' worked over the former Great Central line, and had to tackle Woodhead in the course of her test runs between Marylebone and Manchester; but the only 'foreign' running vouchsafed to the 'King' was between Kings Cross and Leeds.

I do not think I should be far wrong in asserting that there has never been a series of railway events in Great Britain that was subject to more misconstructions being placed on the outward and visible results. In some respects the past history of the Great Western, in its participation in Interchange Trials, was responsible for this. In 1910 *Polar Star* had given some very impressive results on the LNWR; in 1926 *Launceston Castle* did very well between Euston and Carlisle, while in the 1925 exchange with the LNER *Caldicot Castle* and *Pendennis Castle* had run so brilliantly as to cause considerable embarrassment, not to say outright annoyance, to Sir Nigel Gresley. By their most ardent supporters it was confidently expected that the Western Region would 'tear into' the 1948 Interchange Trials in much the same spirit, despite the limited sphere of activity imposed; though why a 'Castle' should have been allowed to run to Carlisle in 1926 and a 'King' was prohibited in 1948 was something of a puzzle. The maximum width over the cylinder cleading was the same on both, namely 8ft 11½in; but perhaps the fundamental differences of ½in in their overall widths over that of the 'Star', which had successfully run to Crewe in 1910, made all the difference! Incidentally, the overall width of the streamlined 'Coronation' 4–6–2s of the LMS was 8ft 10½in. To the chagrin of their sup-

TABLE 41

'KING' CLASS BOILERS

		Original standard	No 6022
Blast pipe, single, jumper top, diameter	in	$5\frac{1}{2}$	$5\frac{1}{4}$
Heating surfaces	sq ft		
tubes		1655.5	1114.0
flues		352.0	704.0
firebox		193.5	194.5
Total evaporative		2201	2012.5
Superheater:			
No of elements		16	32
Heating surface	sq ft	289	489

porters 'on the touchline', however, the Great Western engines, while running to the rather pedestrian schedules of the day, showed little sparkle in their work, and the only modest note of defiance was that the selected engines all bore the initials GW on their tenders, together with the old coat of arms, whereas many of their rivals were newly painted with the legend British Railways on their tenders.

To gain some appreciation of why the Great Western locomotives produced running that was no more than respectably, if adequately, dull, one must look to the personalities involved at the higher levels of engineering management. In the new organisation every post connected with locomotive engineering and running had gone to an ex-LMS man. This is not to suggest that these appointments were anything but well deserved, and I have the highest opinion of the men concerned; but somewhat naturally it resulted, much farther down the scale, in the LMS men entering into the trials with a terrific superiority complex—which incidentally was not reflected either in the day-to-day running, or the results subsequently published by British Railways. The LNER however was caught in the aftermath of the Thompson *débâcle* and, as I have told elsewhere,* did not have too happy a time either.

* LNER Steam

Page 205. (above) *11.10am Paddington–Birkenhead express leaving Gobowen: engine No 1016* County of Hants; *(below) 8.45am Plymouth–Liverpool and Manchester Express at Exeter: engine No 5032* Usk Castle

Page 206. (above) *Down freight train on the Teignmouth sea wall:* ex-ROD *2–8–0 No 3029;* (below) *down fast freight for the South Wales line passing Wootton Bassett: engine No 3856*

The Southern position could have been made very difficult too. O. V. S. Bulleid was, I believe, very disappointed at not securing the top locomotive position on British Railways, and was in no frame of mind to cooperate. An extraordinary degree of security was imposed regarding observation of the work in the trials, and there is a story told that on one occasion when Bulleid, without prior arrangement, went to board the dynamometer car at Waterloo, he was refused admission! But the Southern position was changed utterly through the enthusiasm of W. Pelham Maitland, the running superintendent at Nine Elms shed, who briefed his drivers and firemen to such a degree that they set out to lick the proverbial pants off everybody.

The Great Western management was strongly hostile to nationalisation. Sir James Milne had declined the offer of the chairmanship of the Railway Executive, and A. S. Quartermain likewise refused the offer of membership of the Executive, responsible for civil engineering and signalling. Hawksworth, who held the responsibility for running, as well as for design and workshop matters, was made subservient to the Railway Executive to a degree that former chief mechanical engineers would have found quite intolerable. The post had carried by far the greatest overall responsibility of any railway engineer in Great Britain, and now, during the Interchange Trials, he had to ask permission from the Railway Executive to ride in his own dynamometer car! It is, on reflection, small wonder that the Swindon attitude to the trials was somewhat lukewarm. Of course Sam Ell and his team had a wonderful time testing the locomotives of the other railways, not only on the former GWR routes but also on the Southern; but during the trials they were, to a great extent, detached from their normal allegiances, and working with the newly set-up locomotive testing committee of the Railway Executive as an entirely impartial body. It provided Ell and his men with a breadth of experience with locomotives of other than Great Western design that was to prove invaluable later.

Reverting to the actual running of the Great Western locomotives the drivers concerned were not renowned as record breakers. Russell of Old Oak who took No 6018 *King Henry VI* to the Eastern Region for the Leeds run, and who also

207

worked No 6990 *Witherslack Hall* between Marylebone and Manchester, was a 'safe' painstaking engineman, who timed the trains accurately, but without any attempt at giving even the slightest indication of what the locomotives could really do beyond that demanded by the easy schedules of the day. So close was his timing on most occasions that superficial observers got the impression that he was finding difficulty in maintaining schedules. The important trials of mixed traffic engines between Bristol and Plymouth on the Penzance–Wolverhampton trains led to an extraordinary situation. It was decreed that a Bristol man should work the trains, and it involved lodging overnight at Plymouth. Now Bath Road shed, Bristol, had never worked any lodging trains and there was the strongest opposition to it. It may be recalled that in 1954 there was a strike on the Western Region over the widespread introduction of such duties, and then Bristol was definitely the storm centre. In the normal working of the 'hampton, as the train was known west of Bristol, engines were changed at Newton Abbot, with one engine working through from Wolverhampton. With the workings changed for purposes of the trials one would have thought that with the manning difficulty that developed it could have been turned over to Laira shed, which already had plenty of lodging turns. But the decree persisted, and volunteers were called for. None of the regular express drivers came forward, and the *only* volunteer was a relatively junior man, with little experience on first class work, who had in any case to learn the road west of Newton Abbot. So it was not altogether surprising that the results from the 'Hall' were not very brilliant.

Then there was the vexed question of the coal. It was decreed, naturally enough, that all trials, on whatever region, should be carried out with a uniform grade of coal: Yorkshire 'hards', from South Kirkby Colliery, for the express passenger locomotives, and Blidworth grade 2B for the mixed traffic. In the ordinary way Great Western enginemen would have adapted themselves readily enough to this, as indeed the actual drivers and firemen engaged on the trials did. Generally speaking the engines steamed freely throughout. But the Swindon authorities chose to make something of an issue out of this, so much so that after the main set of Interchange

Trials was concluded a supplementary set was run entirely over Western Region routes with locomotives burning the normal grades of soft Welsh coal. In this comparison the 'King' working the 1.30pm Paddington to Plymouth, and the 8.30am up showed only a slight improvement—an improvement that could amply have been accounted for by the difference between one individual locomotive and another, or between methods of individual drivers; but the work of the 'Hall' No 6961 was as different from that of No 6990 as chalk from cheese. The reason was not hard to find. In the second series No 6961 was worked by a first rate Laira top-link man, Jack Solomon, who I came to know well in later years, and naturally he started with an immense advantage over the sole Bristol 'volunteer'. He brought the basic coal consumption down from 4.11 to 3.22lb per DHP hour! I travelled as a passenger in some of the test trains in the main series of tests between Plymouth and Bristol, and from the general running

TABLE 42

INTERCHANGE TRIALS 1948

Comparative figures of *all* coal used, in relation to *all* work performed, equating the total weight in pounds, against the work done in horsepower hours.

Engine classes	Ratio: $\dfrac{\text{all coal}}{\text{all work}}$
GWR 'King'	3.57
LNER 'A4'	3.06
LMS 'Duchess'	3.12
LMS Converted 'Royal Scot'	3.38
SR Merchant Navy	3.60
GWR 'Hall'	3.94
LNER 'B1'	3.59
LMS Class '5'	3.54
SR West Country	4.11
GWR '28XX' 2–8–0	3.42
LNER 'O1' 2–8–0	3.37
LMS '8F' 2–8–0	3.52
Austerity 2–8–0	3.77
Austerity 2–10–0	3.52

point of view the LNER 'B1' 4–6–0 and the LMS 'Black Five' put up running that was much more impressive than that of *Witherslack Hall*. To show how the Great Western locomotives shaped in comparison with the others I have prepared the accompanying Table 42, and a second Table 43 gives the results for the Marylebone–Manchester trials, when *Witherslack Hall* was being driven by Russell of Old Oak.

TABLE 43

ENGINE NO 6990 *Witherslack Hall*

Great Central Line: Marylebone–Manchester

Length of trip	206.1 miles
Booked running time:	
Down	295min
Up	299min
Load of train, tons tare:	
Down	358.75
Up	375
Actual average speeds:	
Down: 22 June	39.28mph
Up: 23 June	40.3mph
Down: 24 June	40.87mph
Up: 25 June	40.0mph
Coal per dhp hour on four successive trips:	4.28*, 3.62, 4.04, 3.48lb
Average drawbar horsepower while under power:	636, 685, 696, 710

* The high coal consumption on the first down journey was due to poor steaming because of a defective steam pipe joint

The overall results with the mixed traffic engines, including those from the LMS, LNER and Southern representatives over the route where the GWR engine did not run, are shown in the general table. One cannot attach any particular significance to these overall results, in view of the wide variation in attitude displayed by the various engine crews. All that one can say, especially having regard to the circumstances in which the 'Hall' was run between Bristol and Plymouth is that there was not a great deal to choose between them all.

The second series of trials with 'King' class engines were of more significance in a different way. In addition to running a standard engine with Welsh coal instead of Yorkshire 'hards' the opportunity was taken to put the high superheat engine No 6022 through a set of full-dress road tests on the same two trains for comparative purposes. The three sets of trials between Paddington and Plymouth gave the results shown in Table 44.

TABLE 44

'KING' CLASS TRIALS: PADDINGTON–PLYMOUTH

Engine No	6018	6001	6022
Type	Standard	Standard	High Superheat
Coal	Yorkshire hard	Soft Welsh	Soft Welsh
Calorofic Value BTU per lb	14,400	15,100	15,100
COAL			
lb per train mile	48.82	42.28	41.23
lb per DHP hour	3.74	3.33	3.10
WATER			
galls per train mile	36.2	38.7	36.51
lb per DHP hour	27.71	30.46	27.47
lb of water per lb of coal	7.41	9.15	8.86

To get the exact comparison, having regard to the difference in calorific values of the fuels one must take the equivalent figures for Welsh coal, and this raises the values for engines 6001 and 6022 in the ratio of 15,100 to 14,400. The coal per DHP hour of engine No 6022 is thereby increased from 3.10 to 3.25, but still showing a substantial drop from the 3.74lb of engine No 6018.

211

By the kindness of Mr Hawksworth I was able to see No 6022 on the stationary plant at Swindon, and at a later date he arranged for me to ride her on a regular duty, down from Paddington to Plymouth on the 3.30pm express, and back with the up Cornish Riviera Express on the following day. At that time the 3.30pm stopped at Taunton, and the running was not far short of that demanded by pre-war schedules; it must be admitted, however, that the loads out of Paddington were not those regularly conveyed by the Limited in pre-war years. The most impressive part of the down journey lay in the ascent of the South Devon banks and details are given

TABLE 45

WESTERN REGION: EXETER: PLYMOUTH

Load: 7 coaches, 232 tons tare, 250 tons full
Engine: 6022 *King Edward III*

Distance Miles		Sch. min	Actual m	s	Speeds mph
0.0	EXETER	0	0	00	—
4.8	Exminster		6	24	easy
20.1	NEWTON ABBOT	25	25	05	—
23.1	*Milepost 217*		29	15	45
24.1	*Dainton Box*	$32\frac{1}{2}$	30	57	31
28.9	Totnes	$39\frac{1}{2}$	38	30	$47\frac{1}{2}$
30.1	*Milepost 224*		40	05	$44\frac{1}{2}$
31.1	*Milepost 225*		41	42	$35\frac{1}{2}$
32.1	*Milepost 226*		43	25	$34\frac{1}{2}$
33.1	*Milepost 227*		44	52	$42\frac{1}{2}$
33.4	*Rattery Box*	49	45	22	—
35.7	Brent	52	48	25	—
45.3	*Hemerdon Box*	64	61	20	easy
50.5	*Lipson Junction*	71	67	38	
52.0	PLYMOUTH	75	71	12	

On Dainton Bank cut-off increased from 20 per cent to maximum of 33 per cent.
On Rattery Bank cut-off increased from 20 per cent on passing Totnes to 30 per cent from Milepost 225. Reduced to 25 per cent at Milepost 226.

in Table 45 of this part of the run in some elaboration, including notes on the actual engine working. It was an exhilarating experience on the footplate, and gave me a very favourable impression of the increased potentialities given to the 'Kings' by a considerably higher degree of superheating. Returning the following day, with a 12-coach train, we had to take pilot assistance from Plymouth to Newton Abbot, and the non-stop run from Exeter to Paddington is shown in Table 46. It had an amusing prelude. In the conditions of indifferent fuel that so frequently beset express train workings at that time, arrangements were made for men from the shed to board certain express trains at Exeter, and get coal forward, so as to help the fireman on the non-stop run to London. On this trip a young lad duly climbed on and was busily shovelling, while we, on the footplate were chatting about the potentialities of the locomotive, and kindred points of interest. We got the 'rightaway', and suddenly there was a scuffle at the back, and a forgotten though fortunately agile young man came leaping down over the coal, and bade us a hurried farewell as the engine was actually moving. Driver, fireman, inspector and I had all forgotten he was up there!

As to the run itself, with a load of no more than 450 tons, and so good an engine as No 6022, a schedule of 191 minutes, non-stop, for the 173.5 miles to Paddington could have been a mere holiday outing. But Inspector Pullen was anxious to show off the capabilities of the engine, and with the ready and enthusiastic co-operation of driver and fireman we got the kind of performance that Great Western supporters had hoped to see in the Interchange Trials of 1948. By pre-war standards, and indeed by the standards that were set up from 1955 onwards, it was nothing very much out of the ordinary; but with a clear road and nothing remotely extending the engine at any point we sailed into Paddington $8\frac{1}{4}$min early. Because of the unreliability of fuel supplies at that time there was nevertheless a strong undercurrent of resistance, at all levels of the service, to acceleration of train times, and I shall always remember the comment of another driver whom I knew well, when I told him about this run. Hearing about the eight-minutes early arrival in Paddington he shook his head and commented: 'Now, that's giving the show away!'

TABLE 46

WESTERN REGION: EXETER: PADDINGTON
'Cornish Riviera Express'
Load: 13 coaches, 417 tons tare, 450 tons full
Engine: 6022 *King Edward III*

Distance Miles		Sch. min	Actual min	sec
0.0	EXETER	0	0	00
12.6	Cullompton		15	35
19.9	*Whiteball Box*	25	23	58
			pw slack	
30.8	TAUNTON	37	33	25
42.7	*Curry Rivel Junction*		44	45
58.3	CASTLE CARY	65	61	37
65.2	*Brewham Box*		70	17
78.9	*Heywood Rd Junction*	88	84	35
92.4	Patney	102	98	17
103.4	Savernake	114	109	37
120.4	NEWBURY	130	127	04
137.5	READING	148	144	44
155.0	Slough	167	162	20
167.8	Ealing Broadway		174	47
173.5	PADDINGTON	191	182	40

In other words, given favourable conditions they could readily reproduce pre-war speed, yet they were most reluctant to show their hand, lest they were always expected to do it. Nevertheless Hawksworth, in his modifications to engine No 6022, had taken a major step forward towards the provision of locomotives that could be relied upon to provide pre-war standards of running with post-war fuel. The experience Ell gained with this engine was the starting point towards the great revival that took place at Swindon, in British Railways' days, under the leadership of the dynamic Alfred Smeddle.

Before ending this account of Hawksworth's work mention must be made of two new small but significant locomotive designs brought out in the concluding stages of the purely Great Western story. The significance of both was perhaps not quite what their originators intended. And I may add at once that the inspiration, if such it may be called, did not emanate from Swindon in either case. For some years empty stock workings from Old Oak Common into Paddington Station had been almost entirely carried out by the ubiquitous and highly efficient Pannier 0–6–0 tank engines of the '5700' class, and its numerical successors. At times of heavy traffic the express passenger engine of an 'extra' might be utilised, tender first, to take in the stock for a preceeding train, and subsequently to make an easy transition from one platform to an adjoining one. But otherwise the pannier tanks had the job to themselves. Then, in the immediate post-war years, certain directors came to express the view that it hardly improved the 'image' of the company to have so many 'old fashioned' engines, with huge steam domes working in and around Paddington. It availed little, apparently, when it was pointed out that despite their domes the panniers were most efficient engines. Swindon was instructed to produce an 0–6–0 shunting engine with a tapered domeless boiler, and the characteristic Great Western look. This was readily enough produced, by a synthesis of standard parts, using the superheated boiler of the '22XX' class light 0–6–0 tender engine.

TABLE 47

'94xx' CLASS 0–6–0 TANK LOCOMOTIVE

Cylinders: diameter	17½in
stroke	24in
Wheels, diameter	4ft 7½in
Heating surfaces:	
tubes	1069sq ft
firebox	102sq ft
superheater	74sq ft
Grate area	17.4sq ft
Boiler pressure	200lb per sq in
Total weight in working order	55.3ton
Nominal tractive effort	22,515lb

The new class introduced in 1947 was known as the '94XX', and its principal dimensions were as in Table 47.

The second tank engine design was prepared largely at the

instigation of Captain Hugh Vivian, formerly chairman of the locomotive committee of the GWR board, and also chairman of Beyer, Peacock & Co Ltd. I remember his telling me of his great pleasure at getting an engine with outside Walschaerts gear built for the 'GWR' although it did not appear before the old company was swallowed up in British Railways. The first of the class appeared in 1949. At that time it could have been no more than a gesture, a symbol to show that Swindon was 'with it', in the provision of new motive power to suit post-war conditions, when it was highly desirable to have everything 'get-at-able' from outside, without any necessity for placing an engine over a pit. It is, however, doubtful if the new '1500' class had the same ability to lift a heavy train off the mark that was possessed by engines having the standard Swindon setting of the Stephenson link motion, particularly as they were not superheated. Nevertheless the '15XX's took turns with the new '94XX' working empty stock into and out of Paddington. My many footplate runs on Great Western locomotives did not however extend to riding these trains, with which the major feat of haulage was, of course, lifting trains of 400 to 500 tons over the 'flyover' from the Old Oak yards to the empty carriage line south of the main running lines from Ladbroke Grove Box into Paddington. The principal dimensions of the '1500' class are shown in Table 48.

TABLE 48

'15XX' CLASS 0–6–0 TANK LOCOMOTIVE

Cylinders: diameter	17½in
stroke	24in
Wheels, diameter	4ft 7½in
Heating surfaces:	
tubes	1245.7sq ft
firebox	101.7sq ft
Grate area	17.4sq ft
Boiler pressure	200lb per sq in
Total weight in working order	58.2ton
Nominal tractive effort	22,515lb

These locomotives were not superheated

CHAPTER 14

GWR to BR (WR): The Revival

In a book with a title such as *Great Western Steam* there could well be a disposition to ring down the curtain on 31 December, 1947, or at any rate when Mr Hawksworth retired twelve months later. But through the determination and force of personality of certain men the spirit of the old company not only lingered on, but through them, and those who had the task of carrying out their policies, what might be termed the neo-Great Western locomotive practice came to play a very important part in the concluding years of steam on British Railways. With the one outstanding exception of Alfred Smeddle, all those most intimately concerned were ex-Great Western men. This concluding epoch, which flowered so brilliantly from 1953 onwards, entirely with ex-Great Western locomotives, certainly forms an exhilarating final phase of Great Western Steam. Yet it is not a little strange to recall that it took place very largely as a result of the British Railways decision to have done with steam!

While R. A. Riddles was in office, as the member of the Railway Executive responsible for mechanical and electrical engineering, the policy of British Railways so far as motive power was concerned was clear enough. As he expressed it more than once, in the straitened economic circumstances of the country as a whole he was going to use the form of motive power that provided the highest tractive effort per pound sterling—steam. Then he would begin main line electrification as soon as finance was available, so as to utilise our great indigenous source of fuel supply, and avoid using foreign exchange for purchase of fuel oil from overseas. A new range of standard steam locomotive designs was prepared, with some urgency, and it was intended that all future developments should be centred upon these new standards, which incorporated various features then considered to be axiomatic. Then, however, extremely strong pressure, largely from external and non-technical sources, was applied to British Railways to follow the lead of the railways of the USA, and adopt diesel traction. When finance was made available by the government of the day, on a vast scale, for modernisation of British Railways, a major point among the detailed proposals of the plan was the elimination of steam traction. This is no place to discuss the wisdom of the proposal itself, or the steps that were immediately taken to carry it out, but in effect it had a considerable influence upon further events at Swindon. So far as personnel was concerned the changes that had been made since nationalisation had not had quite the effects that had been intended.

While R. A. Riddles was in the chair of mechanical and electrical engineering he strove to create a 'British Railways' outlook, in succession to the old company loyalties. He had lived through the disastrous early years of grouping on the LMS, when loyalties to the North Western, to the Midland, and to the Caledonian, had so frustrated attempts to form a new co-ordinated LMS policy. On British Railways, as the older men like Bulleid and Hawksworth retired, he began to move their immediate successors around. At the same time the responsibilities of the former chief mechanical engineer of the Great Western Railway were split into three: K. J. Cook took locomotives; H. Randle, carriages and wagons, and W. N. Pellow became running superintendent. I have good reason to remember this change because my footplate passes, hitherto arranged with the utmost promptitude by Swindon, henceforth had to be referred to Sir Michael Barrington-Ward at Railway Executive Headquarters. I may add, in all fairness, that they were granted as of old, but it all took much longer The retirement of Arthur Peppercorn from the E&NER in 1952 paved the way for more switches of senior locomotive officers. K. J. Cook went to Doncaster, and in his place came Smeddle, from Darlington via Brighton, at which latter establishment he had been assistant mechanical and electrical engineer.

In the meantime other developments were combining to

force the pace on the locomotive department at Swindon. At the time of nationalisation, when Sir James Milne declined the offer of the chairmanship of the Railway Executive he also retired from railway service, and his former deputy, K. W. C. Grand, was appointed chief regional officer of the newly-formed Western Region. This was a position that, with a far greater degree of autonomy, was later designated general manager. Now Grand was a railwayman as forthright and as proud of the Great Western heritage as ever Sir Felix Pole had been, and he set out to plan for accelerations that would restore the full pre-war standards of speed on all express routes, and would make improvements even upon some of these. Before he left for Doncaster Cook had repeatedly said that the locomotives were ready for such a programme, but no immediate steps had been taken to put this to the proof. But when Grand demanded the restoration of the Bristolian to a $1\frac{3}{4}$-hour schedule for the summer service of 1954 there was consternation among certain senior officers, who could not believe that the locomotives were capable of it. Really one could not blame them. Gilbert Matthews, who had been superintendent of the Line during the latter years of the war, and through the period of austerity that followed, was then operating superintendent of the Western Region. With all the experience of bad steaming, and unreliability of performance he could not share Cook's confidence; and when Smeddle succeeded to the chair at Swindon he was met by the full force of this pessimism from the operating side.

Smeddle was just the man for such a situation. Son of an eminent locomotive engineer of the North Eastern Railway, and bred among locomotives, he was every inch a practical railwayman, and while quickly sensing the 'political' situation that existed on the Western Region he was quick to appraise the merit of the work being done in the experimental department at Swindon, and the traditional excellence of the production in the shops, Within weeks almost of his arrival he was ready to tell the world there was nothing his department could not do. A delighted senior assistant once exclaimed to me: 'He's more Great Western than any of us!' Discussions regarding the acceleration of the Bristolian were at times rather trying, and at one stage when Matthews was taking a particularly dismal view of things Grand exclaimed: 'Well double head the b----- thing, Gilbert!' In the meantime Sam Ell, with the most enthusiastic backing of Smeddle, was engaged on a vital but very simple development. His experience in re-draughting the LMS Class '2' 2–6–0, as mentioned in Chapter 9, gave him a lead towards an important change for the standard express passenger 4–6–0s. He set out to secure pre-war power output, consistently, with post-war qualities of fuel in all its frustrating day-to-day variations; and in so doing he discarded the long-cherished Churchward feature of the jumper top on the blastpipe. That, of course, had been introduced to reduce the draught on the fire when the engine was working hard, and so avoid fire throwing and excessive coal consumption. But in 1952 reliable steaming in all conditions was worth far more than the odd decimal point in basic coal consumption, as measured in pounds per drawbar horsepower hour, and after a series of tests on the stationary plant at Swindon a set of revised proportions for blastpipe and chimney liner were established. The necessary parts could be very simply and cheaply made, and engine No 6001 *King Edward VII* was duly modified.

In the early spring of 1953 I saw for a second time the spectacle of a 'King' running hard on the stationary plant at Swindon. With good coal Ell had boosted the maximum sustained steaming capacity up to the remarkable figure—for a boiler the size of the 'King'—of 33,600lb per hour, making possible a sustained output of more than 2,000 indicated horsepower at 70mph. The tests on the stationary plant were followed by tests on the road between Reading and Stoke Gifford, some with good coal, and some with indifferent. The results amply justified Smeddle's confidence, and re-assured Grand to the extent that authority was given for the alteration of a number of 'King' class engines. A similar alteration was designed for the 'Castles'. By the kindness of Mr Smeddle I had the privilege of riding in the dynamometer car on a day when a maximum output test was planned. The engine was to be steamed at 30,000lb per hour, and on a schedule roughly equal to that of the ordinary South Wales expresses of the day over that part of a route a train of no less than 25 coaches was necessary to absorb the power that would be developed. How that test train was worked I have described in full detail in *Stars, Castles and Kings of the* GWR Part II. I may briefly recapitulate here that on the outward journey we ran the 74.2 miles from Scours Lane Box to Stoke Gifford West in 80min 2sec pass to stop, and on the return made the remarkable times set out in Table 49.

TABLE 49

DYNAMOMETER CAR CONTROLLED ROAD TEST

Load: 25 coaches, 796 tons tare, 798 tons full
Engine: 6001 *King Edward VII*

Distance Miles		Time min	sec	Speeds mph
0.0	Stoke Gifford East Box	0	00	—
6.9	Chipping Sodbury	13	58	45
11.5	Badminton	20	06	45½
21.8	Little Somerford	29	32	78
28.6	Wootton Bassett	35	43	58/56
34.2	Swindon	41	34	60
40.0	Shrivenham	47	00	68
45.0	Uffington	51	24	69
51.1	Wantage Road	56	38	70½
58.4	Didcot	62	48	71
66.7	Goring	70	03	67
70.0	Pangbourne	72	57	67
73.5	Scours Lane Junction	76	55	

Having their tools, so to speak, Ell and his staff set out to draft the point-to-point times for the new accelerated schedules, based not on maximum but for normal steaming rates, and allowing certain definitely prescribed amounts of recovery time to allow for permanent way, and other incidental checks. All this time the 'doubting Thomases' of the operating department remained sceptical, but as more of the modified engines came into traffic the confidence that reigned inside Swindon Works spread to the running staff. One of the first 'Castles' to be altered was No 5025 *Chirk Castle*, and of her a driver once remarked to me: 'She was always a good engine, but now she's an absolute smasher!' This must not be taken in the same sense as the comment of a fireman on one of the new 'Britannia' 4–6–2s that she was 'a *rattling*

221

good engine'! In the early autumn of 1953 I rode engine
No 6001 in regular service on the up Cornish Riviera Express. The train was more sharply timed than when I rode
No 6022 in 1948, but the job was done with supreme ease.
The accompanying log, Table 50, giving no more than a sum-

TABLE 50

WESTERN REGION: EXETER–PADDINGTON

Cornish Riviera Express
Load: 12 coaches, 396 tons tare 430 tons full
Engine: 6001 *King Edward VII*

Distance Miles		Actual min	sec	Speeds mph
0.0	EXETER	0	00*	
3.5	Stoke Canon	4	15	53
12.6	Cullompton	13	30	64½
19.9	*Whiteball*	21	08	47½
23.7	Wellington	24	36	85
—		sigs.		60
30.8	TAUNTON	30	45	64
38.8	Athelney	38	08	67
58.4	Castle Cary	56	30	72/58
65.2	*Brewham*	64	19	44
78.9	*Heywood Road Junction*	77	03	73
86.6	Lavington	84	11	68
92.4	Patney	90	05	56/64
103.4	Savernake	101	30	58
120.4	NEWBURY	117	35	69 (max)
137.5	READING	134	43	—
155.0	Slough	153	07	60 (max)
173.5	PADDINGTON	173	56	

Schedule time 178min
*Times from passing Exeter slowly

mary of the performance, shows excellent timekeeping, and
apart from the climb from Castle Cary to Brewham summit
the reverser was never further forward than 18 per cent.
Then on passing Reading, with things so comfortably in
hand, the driver asked casually 'What would you like now, 60

Page 223. (above) *Through freight to the Southern line traversing the 'old incline' at Reading East: engine, 2–8–2 tank No 7214;* (below) *up freight at Lapworth troughs, hauled by* ex-ROD *2–8–0 locomotive*

Page 224. (above) *Up stopping train near Starcross: engine No 6813* Eastbury Grange; *(below) 11.0am ex-Paddington, West of England express near Sonning. Engine No 1000* County of Middlesex, *in* BR *livery*

or 80?' It was as easy as that. But as the log shows we were already ahead of time, and Inspector Pullen and I regretfully had to say 'sixty'. Otherwise we might once again have startled Paddington with an exceptionally early arrival.

My second trip on one of the modified engines was on the heavier 8.30am up, the 'Dutchman', with engine No 6023 *King Edward II*. It was another very competent display, but I will refer to it only in another respect, that of the riding qualities of Great Western locomotives at high speed. With but few exceptions I have found them all, 'Kings', 'Castles', 'Stars', 'Saints' and 'Halls' alike, very steady, but on this occasion Driver Solomon gave us a most interesting exposition down the Wellington bank. Now the steep descent from Whiteball Tunnel towards Taunton is not a completely ideal racing ground. The curves are gradual it is true, but they are practically continuous one way or the other from the tunnel exit until a good half way between Wellington and Norton Fitzwarren stations. If an engine began to rock or sway a most dangerous condition could be set up at high speed. I have known 'Castles' in quite first class condition give nasty rolls on this descent. But No 6023 was taken down the bank in terrific style, reaching a maximum of 92mph, but riding so plumb-steady that I was able to take my notes standing with scarcely a touch of the cab sides, as we elegantly rode the curves one after another. I have no doubt that the *City of Truro* was riding very steadily when she made her record descent in May 1904. When I rode her in 1957 and she was taken up to 84mph she was as steady as No 6023; but I can't imagine that her outside-cylindered counterparts of the 'County' class were so comfortable on this stretch of line.

By the early spring of 1954 preparations for the restoration of the 1¾-hour Bristolian were well advanced, and arrangements were made in April for a demonstration run—not for publicity purposes but finally to convince the operating department that Swindon had appropriate tools for the job. So arrangements were made for a dynamometer car test run that would provide a round trip considerably more severe than the actual service train would entail. The special was timed to leave Paddington at 10.55am, run in the Bristolian's point-to-point times to the outskirts of Bristol, but then, instead of going into Temple Meads station, to take the northward curve at North Somerset Junction and call briefly at Stapleton Road before returning at Bristolian speed to Paddington via Badminton. It was to be an almost continuous run, at high speed, over a distance of 230 miles. Furthermore, no special arrangements were made for the allocation of a locomotive in good condition. All that was laid down was that it must be a 'King' with improved draughting, and the first top link crew that was spare on that day was put on to the job. I had an invitation to ride in the dynamometer car, and recorded the following remarkable running. Leaving at 10.55am we were back in Paddington at 2.29pm, and the summary details of our progress are shown in Table 52. Our running averages were 71.7mph from Paddington to Dr Day's Bridge Junction, and 73mph from Stapleton Road to Paddington. The aggregate of 233.9 miles was overed in 195 minutes at an average speed of 72.2mph, and the entire round trip of 235 miles, including two stops in the Bristol district and proceeding slowly between the two, gave the remarkable overall average speed of 66mph from Paddington to Paddington, via Stapleton Road.

So the Bristolian went into regular service and in the very first week a new record was made with engine No 6015 *King Richard III* in running the up train from Temple Meads to Paddington in 95min start-to-stop, average 74mph. But Grand had only just started on his programme of acceleration, and the next item was the restoration of a four-hour service between Paddington and Plymouth with the Cornish Riviera Express. All the old arguments started again. The 'Kings' were no longer up to the job, according to the operating department, and it was seriously suggested that engines might be hired from another region. It so happened also that the one-and-only 'BR8' three-cylinder express passenger 'Pacific' was on test at Swindon, and her potentialities were unofficially compared to those of the 'Kings'. So Smeddle, who had had a long experience of testing work with the Darlington dynamometer car, proposed to run a series of trials with Class '8' locomotives on the Cornish Riviera Express, and opened negotiations for borrowing 'Pacifics' from the Eastern and the London Midland Regions. From the former he was very anxious to try a Peppercorn 'A1'. It so happened that the motive power superintendent of the Eastern Region, E. D. Trask, was the very man who, in 1925, had been in charge of the visiting LNER 'Pacific' No 4474 in the Interchange Trials, and from his previous experience he was not keen to release one of his 'A1s' for this purpose. The London Midland were ready enough to co-operate, and a Stanier 4–6–2 No 46237 *City of Bristol* was lent to the Western Region. At one time it was also intended to include the 'BR8' 4–6–2 No 71000 *Duke of Gloucester* in the trials, but Ell had enough data from his tests on the Swindon stationary plant to be able to plot the performance of this engine without making a run at all.

So the only engines to make actual runs with the dynamometer car on the Cornish Riviera Express were the LMR *City of Bristol* and No 6013 *King Henry VIII*. In complete contrast to all other Interchange Trials the LMR engine was worked by Western men, after a sufficient time of running with it to gain familiarity. Furthermore, the ordinary link workings were not changed, and with both the 'King' and the 'Duchess' four different crews were involved in each week: Old Oak men down on the Tuesday and Thursday, Laira men up on the Wednesday and Friday. The loads were made up to twelve coaches between Paddington and Plymouth in each direction, and required double-heading between Newton Abbot and Plymouth. In the down direction conveyance of the Westbury slip portion provided a load of 'fourteen' for the first 95 miles. The trials of the 'King' and the 'Duchess' were carried out with a considerable interval between them, and so far as I could ascertain the crews concerned were not aware that comparative trials were actually being made. But the fact that two different engine sheds were involved in this tough assignment of getting to and from Plymouth in the even four hours led to competitive running of a different kind, as when No 6013 *King Henry VIII* stopped in Newton Abbot in 186¼min from Paddington, 5¾min early on the accelerated schedule, and the fireman climbing down to assist in the coupling on of the bank engine said: 'There, see what the Cockneys can do!'

The last two runs of engine No 6013 on Thursday 10 March and Friday 11 March were two of the hardest ever achieved by engines of this class. In *Stars, Castles and Kings* Part II I have analysed the performance in some detail; but the results were enough to convince the operating department that the 'Kings' were still able to do the job, particularly as No 6013 was not in the best of condition at the time of the tests. On

TABLE 51

CORNISH RIVIERA EXPRESS: 11 MARCH 1955

Dynamometer Car Test Run

Load: 12 coaches, 393 tons tare, 420 tons full
Engine: 6013 *King Henry VIII*
Made against strong easterly wind

Distance Miles		Actual min sec*	Speeds mph
0.0	EXETER	0 00	10
12.6	Cullompton	13 34	65
19.9	*Whiteball Box*	20 38	53½
23.7	Wellington	23 52	80
30.8	TAUNTON	29 27	71/74
38.8	Athelney	35 45	77½
48.0	Somerton	43 29	65
58.4	CASTLE CARY	52 31	75/53†
—		pw slack	17
65.2	*Brewham Box*	63 32	42
78.9	*Heywood Bridge Junction*	75 02	81/70†
86.6	Lavington	81 28	76
92.1	Patney	86 41	64½
98.2	Pewsey	91 41	73
103.4	Savernake	96 20	61
120.4	NEWBURY	111 43	80
126.7	Midgham	116 52	58†
132.3	Theale	121 46	74½
137.5	READING	127 45	37†
155.0	Slough	143 07	74½
167.8	Ealing Broadway	153 51	70
—		sigs	
173.5	PADDINGTON	162 04	

* Times from passing Exeter slowly
†Speed restrictions

the down journey, when we had passed Taunton in 130¼min from the start, 6¼min early, Smeddle sat down beside me in the dynamometer car chuckling, and said: 'Even old Gilbert's smiling now!' Hearing afterwards about what had transpired I was very sorry not to have been able to accept Smeddle's

TABLE 52

HIGH SPEED TEST RUN: 30 APRIL 1954

Load: 8 coaches, 253 tons tare, 260 tons full
Engine: 6003 *King George IV*

Distance Miles		Sch min	Actual min sec	Speeds mph
0.0	PADDINGTON	0	0 00	—
9.1	Southall	11	10 18	72
18.5	Slough	17½	17 51	75
36.0	READING	31	31 23	82/74*
53.1	Didcot	48	44 44	84
66.5	Uffington		54 38	79½
—			pw slack	18
77.3	SWINDON	67	65 44	72
87.7	Dauntsey		73 20	96½
94.0	CHIPPENHAM	79	77 33	78
101.9	Box		83 30	82
106.9	BATH	88½	88 17	35*
117.9	*Dr Day's Bridge Junction*	102½	99 19	
0.0	STAPLETON ROAD	0	0 00	—
16.0	Badminton	18	17 47	66/63
26.3	Little Somerford		25 25	93
33.1	Wootton Bassett	30½	30 22	65*
38.7	SWINDON	35½	35 03	79
62.9	Didcot	56	51 52	92½
80.0	READING	68	64 31	77*
97.5	Slough	81	77 08	90/81*
110.3	Ealing Broadway		86 53	77
—			pw slack	
116.0	PADDINGTON	101½	95 35	

* Speed restrictions

invitation to accompany the up test run on the following day, but unfortunately I had business upon the North East Coast, and had to return from Plymouth to Paddington on the 4.10 pm express on the Thursday. So far as the making of record times was concerned it was unfortunate that a very strong easterly wind was blowing on the Friday, and those twelve coaches of the test train were pulling like fifteen, or even more. Consequently a most exceptional effort had to be made to maintain the four-hour schedule, and the engine performance, as shown in Table 51, was an outstanding effort by the Laira crew concerned, Driver Bolt and Fireman Knapman.

In the meantime the Swindon testing staff had been obtaining much very valuable information in the stationary plant trials of the 'BR8' 'Pacific' No 71000, which, it will be recalled had a twin-orifice blastpipe that was precisely to the dimensions of the Dean Goods 0-6-0—two '2301' blastpipes side by side. Ell was so impressed with the way in which the twin blastpipe freed up the exhaust that he persuaded Smeddle to allow him to work out a twin blastpipe design for a 'King'. The proportion did not work out quite satisfactorily on the first engine so fitted, No 6007, but with No 6015 *King Richard III* equipped in 1955 Ell scored an absolute bulls-eye! It was very unfortunate that when dynamometer car tests came to be run with an engine that was later equipped in the same way, namely No 6002 *King William IV*, the weather conditions in early summer were as near perfect as one could imagine, and the up journey which had extended No 6013 almost to the limit was made to look a simple task, and the comparative figures of coal consumption and power output give no idea that the same train was being worked (see Table 53).

Despite the onset of the diesel programme it then seemed likely that steam would have to carry on for some considerable time, and not only was authority obtained to convert all the 'Kings' to the twin-orifice blastpipe arrangement, but the principle was also applied to many of the 'Castles' and the 'County' class 4-6-0s. From the viewpoint of historical records it is a pity that no 'all-out' trials were conducted with any of these engines extending them to the same extent that No 6013 was extended in March 1955, with the making of fully comprehensive tests on the stationary plant as No 6001 was tested

TABLE 53

UP CORNISH RIVIERA TESTS

Year	1955	1956
Engine No	6013	6002
Type of blastpipe	Single	Double
Load (tons tare)	393½	391
Average speed (mph)	64.7	64.7
Weather	Strong adverse wind	Fine
Firing rate lb/hr	4210	2800
Net steam rate per hr	29835	20800
Average dhp	1020	799
Coal per dhp hr (lb) exclusive of auxiliaries	4.0	3.5

in 1952-3. But by the year 1956 Swindon was very fully occupied with the problems of the new diesels, and the time of steam locomotive development had come virtually to an end.

CHAPTER 15

In Retrospect: An Appraisal

AMONG Great Western supporters I have met those to whom any suggestion of criticism of the old company or indication that other places than Swindon also had their share in the advancement of steam locomotive engineering was sheer sacrilege. I shall always remember the fury of a reader of a certain monthly journal who cancelled his subscription because I had dared to criticise one feature of Great Western locomotive performance, and refused to retract in response to his irate letters! However, to appreciate the immense strength of Swindon locomotive practice it is essential to take heed of the other side of the coin. In taking a final look here at one of the most impressive steam locomotive developments in history it is evident that there were some weak, if not necessarily missing, links in the chain. But before doing so, I cannot forbear to comment upon a new and unexpected development in the Swindon locomotive story. It is not a development in design, but one of utilisation. In the very week I was writing this concluding chapter the British Railways' ban on the running of preserved steam locomotives was lifted, partially at any rate; and one of the great stars of this particular saga, No 6000 *King Geaorge V*, was permitted to leave seclusion at Hereford, and to take the road once more.

While it is good news that steam hauled trips are likely to be possible once again, and that historic locomotives like the *Pendennis Castle*, and other Great Western celebrities may become *living* memorials to a great age, instead of so many static museum pieces, it does not, of course, alter the story of Great Western locomotive development in practice—a story that has been concluded now for many years. It is the twentieth-century development to which I am referring, and looking at it in retrospect, and dissecting the phases one from another, one can discern where the weaknesses as well as the strength lay. It comes as something of a shock perhaps to recall that the first phase, which was probably the most vital of all, was completed by the year 1913 by the construction of the 'Prince' series of four-cylinder 4-6-0s having for the first time 15in diameter cylinders, and a nominal tractive effort increased thereby to 27,800lb. These five locomotives, and the fifteen 'Princesses' that followed, marked the consumation of all Churchward's designing and constructional practice at Swindon, and were, without any doubt, the finest express passenger locomotives running the rails in Great Britain at that time. It is true that by the time of grouping the Great Western could not claim the highest recorded output of indicated and drawbar horsepower, that distinction being held until 1922 by the London & North Western 'Claughton' class 4-6-0 No 1159 *Ralph Brocklebank*; but in all-round consistency of performance the Churchward 'Stars' were pre-eminent.

It was the principles and detailed features contributing to this pre-eminence that dominated the next phase, which covered the entire Collett régime. In striking contrast to the intensely dynamic atmosphere of the 1903 to 1912 decade it was a period of almost complete stagnation, so far as locomotive developments were concerned. Some readers may wonder whether I am going slightly crazy in applying the term 'stagnation' to a period that saw the introduction of such famous new locomotive classes as the 'Castles' and the 'Kings'. But neither of these classes incorporated any new features of design, other than those necessitated by enlargement. The 'Kings' especially were a clever and successful piece of drawing office work, and many new manufacturing techniques were applied in their construction; but all the new developments lay along the lines of finer and more accurate production. The development of the new standard two-cylinder 'engine' was even more a direct derivative from Churchward's 'Saint' class. Without being in the least derogatory towards the work of Swindon one can safely assert that the 'King' was no more than a greatly enlarged version of a design of 1913.

In continuing the practice of Churchward in the enlarged four-cylinder 4-6-0s of the 'Castle' and 'King' classes, Collett at first took the Great Western as many strides ahead of all other British companies as Churchward had been with the final version of the 'Stars' in 1913. The performances of both the Collett types were superb, and there seemed no need to make any changes as new express passenger locomotives were needed in replacement of older units. It was at this stage that Swindon began to fall behind. In the period of intense development of the steam locomotive all over the world, in the age of Chapelon, in the age when designers were giving the closest study to the internal characteristics of the steam circuit, Swindon continued to build 'Castles' to the original drawings and 'Halls' that were no more than a 6ft version of the Churchward 'Saints'. In what may be termed the rarefied atmosphere of the GWR in the 1930s the newest engines did admirable work, but there was a rough world of railways building up outside those favoured precincts, and World War II brought the walls down with a crash. In the rapidly changing circumstances Swindon locomotives were at a disadvantage in two ways. The first, which was immediate, was the moderate degree of superheat favoured by Churchward. The second weakness was more subtle, and did not show itself very seriously until post–war acceleration was introduced on a big scale.

Churchward adopted a moderate degree of superheat for reasons of thermal efficiency. He disliked the idea of throwing away valuable heat in the exhaust, and so designed his boilers, superheaters and cylinders that with correct expansion of the steam in the cylinders there would be very little superheat left in the steam at exhaust. This pre–supposed that the rated boiler pressure would be constantly maintained, and that the range of expansion as provided by the cut-off used by the driver would result in the designed exhaust pressure. It required skilful firing, but Great Western enginemen had been trained in the craft for upwards of forty years, and generally the traditional scheme of things worked out exactly according to plan. But once conditions of fuel or something else gave rise to a drop in pressure they were in trouble, and it was to meet such difficulties that Hawksworth began to move away from the moderate superheat concept. In this the GWR was far behind the other British railways. Gresley had achieved outstanding success by putting an exceptionally high degree of superheat on to the Great Northern large-boilered 'Atlantics', and the development of his 'Pacifics' followed the same course. Stanier tried Swindon methods when he first went to the LMS, but very soon had to change, and Bulleid put very large super-heaters on his 'Pacifics'. From being a leader the Great West-ern was having to catch up.

When the systematic testing of various pre-nationalisation locomotives was in progress on one or another of the station-ary plants, and dynamometer tests were being run in closely controlled conditions the extent to which the Swindon types were handicapped by their traditional front ends became ap-parent. The Churchward front ends had been peerless in their day, but the design had remained unaltered while other ad-ministrations were developing the priceless attribute of inter-nal streamlining, and making their locomotives much freer running in consequence. After the dynamometer car tests of 1955 on the Cornish Riviera Express with engine No 6013 the limitations of the 'King' in conditions of maximum output were apparent in the diminishing return of power output in relation to steam production, and it was then that the experi-ments with twin-orifice blastpipes began. But what was really needed was a re-design of the cylinders and steam passages on Chapelon principles. A design had already been worked out in connection with the proposed 'Pacific', but it would have required a new set of patterns and tooling, and at that late stage in the history of the Swindon steam locomotive the capi-tal cost of such new equipment would have been too great. The twin-orifice blastpipe freed the engines up considerably, but an immeasurably greater improvement might have been achieved with thoroughly re-designed cylinders, valves, and steam passages.

In one vital respect Swindon never lost its supremacy, and that was in boiler design. The deficiency in superheating was a matter that could be rectified, as Hawksworth showed with his modification to engine No 6022, and the evaporation rates attained in maximum output tests, when related to the heat-ing surface and grate area, easily surpassed those of contem-porary designs on other British railways. Had such steaming capacity been combined with a thoroughly modern front end the results might indeed have been phenomenal. At one stage

Smeddle proposed to improve the 'Kings' still further by putting a batch of them on roller bearings. The necessary parts were actually ordered and were received at Swindon, but the work of conversion was not carried out. I have, however, written enough in the immediately preceeding chapter to show how great a revival in the fortunes of the Swindon locomotive stud took place in the years from 1953 onwards. Smeddle had well-designed and accurately built locomotives to work upon, and Ell's modifications to the draughting certainly put the road performance back to the standards of pre-war days.

Index

237

Index